# ACHIEVING

## YOUR

# MISSION

# ACHIEVING
## YOUR *Life*
# MISSION

## RANDAL A. WRIGHT

**CFI**
**Springville, Utah**

This is not an official publication of The Church of Jesus Christ of Latter-day Saints. The opinions and views expressed herein belong solely to the author and do not necessarily represent the opinions or views of Cedar Fort, Inc. Permission for the use of sources, graphics, and photos is also solely the responsibility of the author.

ISBN 13: 978-1-59955-348-1

Published by CFI, an imprint of Cedar Fort, Inc.
2373 W. 700 S., Springville, UT, 84663
Distributed by Cedar Fort, Inc., www.cedarfort.com

Library of Congress Cataloging-in-Publication Data

Wright, Randal A.
  Achieving your life mission / Randal A. Wright.
    p. cm.
  Includes bibliographical references.
  ISBN 978-1-59955-348-1
  1. Vocation--Church of Jesus Christ of Latter-day Saints. I. Title.

  BV4740.W75 2009
  248.4'89332--dc22

                          2009018918

Cover design by Angela D. Olsen
Cover design © 2009 by Lyle Mortimer

Printed in the United States of America

10 9 8 7 6 5 4 3 2 1

Printed on acid-free paper

# CONTENTS

# INTRODUCTION

———⊰⊱⊰⊱⊰⊱———

This book was born on the night my first child came into the world and has since been more than three decades in the making.

On September 20, 1973, my wife, Wendy, had been in the early stages of labor at home for more than thirty-five hours. Totally exhausted, she was finally admitted to Utah Valley Hospital in Provo, Utah. I was an undergraduate student majoring in business at Brigham Young University at the time and was unsure of what I wanted to do with my life. My impending fatherhood ramped up my uncertainty that night. Sitting beside my wife and watching the monitors attached to her body, I tried to interpret the data I saw on the screen. Even to my untrained eye, something didn't seem right. I found a nurse who confirmed my suspicions; the doctor had already been summoned to come immediately. My fears intensified when a Latter-day Saint doctor arrived and asked me if I wanted to give my wife a priesthood blessing. He assisted with the blessing and then explained that Wendy would need an emergency caesarean section. My weeks of Lamaze training flew out the window. Instead of being by Wendy's side as her coach, I was banished to a small waiting room while she was wheeled into surgery.

Alone in that waiting room and 1,500 miles from any family, I began to pray for help and comfort. I picked up a Book of Mormon that was lying on a small table and began to read. I had always loved this great book of scripture, but reading it during that anxious time took on a different meaning. That night I began to realize that the stories told in the Book of Mormon were not so different from the stories of our lives today. Some people were always righteous; others were the "very vilest of sinners" (Mosiah 28:4) before they repented. Although the major writers lived in different circumstances during the 1,000-year period the record covers, I was struck by something I had in common with them. They all had learned powerful lessons from their life experiences. But unlike me, they tirelessly recorded those experiences and lessons on metal plates for people who would follow. I realized also that they all had very specific missions to perform in life and that many of them had figured out what those missions were and had put them into succinct statements:

- **Nephi:** "For the fulness of mine intent is that I may *persuade* men to come unto the God of Abraham, and the God of Isaac, and the God of Jacob, and be saved" (1 Nephi 6:4, emphasis added).
- **Jacob:** "Wherefore we labored diligently among our people, that we might *persuade* them to come unto Christ, and partake of the goodness of God, that they might enter into his rest" (Jacob 1:7, emphasis added).
- **Mormon:** "And I would that I could *persuade* all ye ends of the earth to repent and prepare to stand before the judgment-seat of Christ" (Mormon 3:22, emphasis added).

I wondered if I had a "mission" to perform on earth. I wasn't sure what it might be, but I made a stab at it. That night in 1973, I made a specific commitment to the Lord: If he allowed Wendy and our baby to live, I would make it my life's mission to study successful families, incorporate the things I learned in my own family, and then share the information with others. I'm not in the habit of bargaining with the Lord, but that night my fear made me desperate. Nearly three hours passed as I anxiously waited. Finally, the doctor brought news that after a difficult Caesarean-section delivery, my wife and baby Nathan were doing well. I silently thanked Heavenly Father and reaffirmed my promise.

It didn't take long for me to act on that promise. I returned to class at BYU the next day, and one of my professors commented that his father had given him a blessing every year of his life on his birthday. This adult son still returned to receive a blessing from his father every year, even though he had eight children of his own. There it was, a life lesson about how a successful family functioned. I wrote it down, and was so impressed that I started the same tradition in my family.

After that night, my focus in school began to change. Even though I was still very interested in business, I added family studies to my undergraduate degree. Those classes became the ones I enjoyed most. Later, when I decided to get a master's degree, I didn't agonize over the area of focus; of course, it would be family studies. Later, when the opportunity arose to pursue a doctorate, there was no doubt in my mind about the subject. During that night in the hospital waiting room and the next day in the BYU class, a love for studying families was born. Since then I have recorded hundreds of experiences and lessons learned about families. I never tire of studying families and try to share what I have learned with others. I am passionate about the subject.

Is there something you feel passionate about and never tire of? If so, it may be related to your unique purpose on earth. If you can't specifically answer that question, this book will help you discover the mission you were sent to perform. One thing is certain. You were saved to come forth at this time of the earth's history for a reason. What is that reason?

# CHAPTER 1

❧❧❧

# You Have a Life
# Mission to Perform

*No man is ever born into the world whose work is not born with*
*him. Everyone has a job to be done which he is supposed to do and*
*which he can do better than anyone else in the world.*
—James Russell Lowell

A story is told about a little boy who tried out for the school
play. He was excited about his chance to be in the spotlight. His
mother took him to the door of the school and then waited outside while
he auditioned for a group of teachers. It seemed only a few minutes
had passed when the boy ran out the door and into his mother's arms,
whooping with excitement about the part he had won. The mother was
pleased that the teachers apparently had recognized her son's potential.
What was the part he would play? "I get to sit in the *front row* and clap
and cheer for the kids on the stage!"

Although the performance is in vain without the audience, far too
many people are satisfied to sit in the front row of life's theater, clapping
and cheering for those who play the real roles on the world's stage. In
the premortal battle we did not choose to come to earth just to clap
and cheer. We learned there that we would have starring roles—not bit
parts—to play in mortality. None of us was sent here to be an extra.

Abraham was told about these roles: "And God saw these souls
that they were good, and he stood in the midst of them, and he said:
These I will make my rulers; for he stood among those that were spirits,
and he saw that they were good; and he said unto me: Abraham, thou

1

art one of them; thou wast chosen before thou wast born" (Abraham 3:23).

The term we use in the Church to describe being chosen in the premortal existence to do an important work on earth is called foreordination. "Foreordination is the premortal selection of individuals to come forth in mortality at specified times, under certain conditions, and to fulfill predesignated responsibilities."[1] Some may confuse foreordination with predestination. However, from a Latter-day Saint point of view, these terms are very different. Predestination means that because of God's foreknowledge, our destinies were cast in stone before we were born. Elder Neal A. Maxwell clarified the doctrine: "Foreordination is like any other blessing—it is a conditional bestowal subject to our faithfulness. Prophecies foreshadow events without determining those outcomes, because of a divine foreseeing of that outcome. So foreordination is a conditional bestowal of a role, responsibility, or a blessing that, likewise, foresees but does not fix the outcome."[2]

# I AM A CHILD OF GOD

A lifelong member of the Church will sing, "I Am a Child of God"[3] hundreds of times. If you believe the lyrics—"I am a child of God, and *He* has sent *me* here"—then you also believe that:

- you lived with our Heavenly Father before you came to this life
- you are his spirit child and he loves you
- you were sent to earth on a special mission that was customized for you

The great questions of the ages come with appropriate Latter-day Saint answers: Who am I? *A child of God.* Where did I come from? *The premortal existence, where I lived with my Heavenly Parents.* Why am I here? *To gain a body, to be tested, to marry and have a family.* While these answers are true, they are universal in their application to all mankind. The real question is not about the entire human race. It is about me. Who am *I*? Where did *I* come from? Why am *I* here? What is *my* special mission here on earth?

The dictionary defines the word mission as "sent out to perform a special duty." Imagine for a moment your premortal state where that mission was proposed. The plan of salvation was presented, and Jesus Christ, the firstborn of the Eternal Father, willingly stepped forward to fill the role of Savior and Redeemer. Perhaps in that world we also became aware of other special assignments given to the giants, such as Jeremiah: "Before I formed thee in the belly I knew thee; and before thou camest forth out of the womb I sanctified thee, and I ordained thee a prophet unto the nations" (Jeremiah 1:4–5). Were we told about the missions of these other spiritual leaders?

- *Adam and Eve*: to be the first parents
- *Noah:* to preach repentance in the face of great wickedness, and then start the family of man all over again
- *Abraham:* to be the father of nations and make an important covenant
- *Moses:* to set his people free from bondage and lead them to a land of promise.
- *Mary:* to be the mother of the Savior of the world
- *Moroni:* to compile the Book of Mormon record and deliver it to Joseph Smith
- *Joseph Smith:* to translate the Book of Mormon, restore the true Church, build temples, and publish revelations
- *Gordon B. Hinckley:* to be the greatest temple builder in the history of the world

Did others receive different kinds of calls?

- *Alexander Bell:* to invent the telephone and help the world communicate
- *Philo Farnsworth*: to invent the television and thereby help spread the gospel to the world
- *Mother Teresa*: to minister to the poor, orphaned, sick, and dying of Calcutta

If we were aware of the mission assignments for the Lord's leaders, then surely we would have assumed that the assignments did not stop there. It is hard to imagine that God would call a meeting with the rest of us and say, "OK, you're not the noble and great ones, but you do get to go down and clap and cheer while the chosen ones do the heavy lifting." That assignment would not have caused such enthusiasm that, "The morning stars sang together, and all the sons of God shouted for joy" (Job 38:7).

Elder Bruce R. McConkie explained what really happened: "To carry forward his own purposes among men and nations, the Lord foreordained chosen spirit children in pre-existence and assigned them to come to earth at particular times and places so that they might aid in furthering the divine will. These pre-existence appointments made 'according to the foreknowledge of God the Father' (1 Peter 1:2.), simply designated certain individuals to perform missions which the Lord in his wisdom knew they had the talents and capacities to do."[4]

There is no doubt that we were saved to come forth at this time of the earth's history to perform a special mission. President Ezra Taft Benson taught, "You have been born at this time for a sacred and glorious purpose. It is not by chance that you have been reserved to come to earth in this last dispensation of the fulness of times. Your birth at this particular time was foreordained in the eternities."[5]

# WHAT IS YOUR ROLE?

In 1990, I was asked to direct a session of the Especially for Youth (EFY) program in Williamsburg, Virginia. It was an honor since this would be the first session ever held in the eastern United States. I wondered why I was chosen for this special assignment. Many of my friends who worked with the program would have loved to direct this landmark session. There was a change in the program that year. For the first time, the session director was assigned to speak at the Thursday night fireside right before the small-group testimony meetings. At past EFY sessions, a musical fireside presented by a popular Latter-day Saint entertainer typically filled the time. However, I felt equal to the task, prepared my talk for that night far in advance and was ready.

Early in the week, as I interacted with the teenagers attending the session, I became aware of the isolation many of them felt in their hometowns, far from any large population center of the Church. A convert from Mississippi said that when she joined the Church a few years earlier, all of her friends rejected her. They said she was joining a "white" church and that she was turning away from her racial heritage. She told how hard it was to have no close friends at school who understood her heart. Then she bore her testimony of the truthfulness of the gospel. She said she told her former friends that she "would be there for them if they ever needed her." Then she said something very quietly, "So far, they have never needed me, but I will be there for them if they ever do."

I talked to others who were the only members of the Church in their high schools, and they wondered if they could stay strong. The more I talked to them, the more pressure I felt to produce a meaningful experience at that fireside. I knew we had one week together and that I would probably never see them again. By Thursday afternoon I was in turmoil. I had torn up my prepared talk and thrown it away. What could I say to teens whose special life missions were so different from their peers who grew up surrounded by supportive Latter-day Saint friends? I prayed for help but no ideas came.

Finally, I asked one of the EFY counselors if he would give me a priesthood blessing. We went into the small dorm room where I was staying, and he laid his hands on my head. I remember well what he said: "There are many who would love to have the opportunity you are having this week." I knew that, since some of my colleagues had brazenly asked me why I had received the plum assignment to go to the College of William and Mary that week. Then he said, "There are many who are qualified to be here in your position." I realized that all of those colleagues were much more qualified than I was to be there. And then he said the words that still play in my head after all these years: "But the Lord wants you to be here this week." Those words sank deeply into my soul. After the blessing, I thanked the counselor and he left. I then sank onto the bed and cried harder than I ever had before. With a clarity I had never experienced, I knew my Heavenly Father was aware of *me* as an individual and that I had a role to play on earth. I knew he was aware of every teenager at EFY that week, and that they also had special missions.

That night at the fireside I spoke about the importance of gaining a testimony of the gospel, and I told them that each of them had a specific mission to perform on earth. I don't remember all that was said, but I know the Spirit was there that night in a remarkable way.

Sixteen years later at the 2006 Campus Education Week in Provo, a woman came up to me and introduced herself as Andrea. She had been one of those teens in Williamsburg whom the Lord knew intimately. "Do you remember the Thursday night fireside in Virginia?" she asked. I assured her that I did. She then said, "I will never forget that night." I told her I would never forget it either.

## EXAMPLES OF THOSE
## REALIZING THEIR MISSIONS

We each have a responsibility to discover our own mission in life. The Savior set the example for us by discovering early on what his mission would be. Elder Joseph B. Wirthlin said, "The Savior prepared for his *life mission* for thirty years. At the age of twelve, he was aware of *his mission*. . . . His ministry lasted only three years, but what he accomplished in those three short years was a miracle and has influenced hundreds of millions of people throughout the world for two centuries."[6]

Joseph Smith also knew early on that he was to be the prophet of the last dispensation. He said, "My grandfather, Asael Smith, long ago predicted that there would be a prophet raised up in his family, and my grandmother was fully satisfied that it was fulfilled in me. My grandfather Asael died . . . after having received the Book of Mormon, and read it nearly through; and he declared that I was the very prophet that he had long known would come in his family."[7]

No Latter-day Saint would doubt that Joseph Smith, Hyrum Smith, Brigham Young, John Taylor, and Wilford Woodruff had special missions to accomplish at a critical time during this last dispensation. But in a revelation given to Joseph F. Smith recorded in Doctrine and Covenants 138: 55–56, we read that they were not the only ones chosen: "I observed that they were also among the noble and great ones who were chosen in the beginning to be rulers in the Church of God. Even before they were born, they, *with many others, received their first lessons in the world of spirits and were prepared to come forth in the due time of the Lord* to labor in his vineyard for the salvation of the souls of men" (emphasis added).

Who are the "many others" who were chosen in the world of spirits? Joseph Smith said, "*Every man* who has a calling to minister to the inhabitants of the world was ordained to that very purpose in the Grand Council of heaven before this world was."[8] The Lord's definition of "man" is found in Doctrine and Covenants 20:18: "And that he created *man, male and female*, after his own image and in his own likeness" (emphasis added). Surely you are one of those who received a call to minister to the inhabitants of the world and were ordained to that purpose in the Grand Council. The only question to answer is what your special mission entails.

Those who are called to do the work of ministering to the "inhabitants of the world" were given that responsibility in the premortal existence. But what about all of the other critical support roles that were required to make it happen? If planes are needed to carry missionaries around the world, then Orville and Wilbur Wright were needed to perform a special mission, too. If General Conference needs to be broadcast worldwide, then Philo Farnsworth needed to step up and help perfect television.

President Spencer W. Kimball taught this important truth regarding women, as well as men, "Remember, in the world before we came here, faithful women were given certain assignments while faithful men were foreordained to certain priesthood tasks. While we do not now remember the particulars, this does not alter the glorious reality of what we once agreed to. You are accountable for those things which long ago were expected of you just as are those we sustain as prophets and apostles. . . . This leaves much to be done by way of parallel personal development—for both men and women." General Relief Society President Julie Beck said, "Women have distinct assignments given to them from before the foundation of the world."[10]

Elder Neal A. Maxwell also commented on the special role of women: "Just as certain men were foreordained from before the foundations of the world, so were certain women appointed to certain tasks. Divine design—not chance—brought Mary forward to be the mother of Jesus. The boy prophet, Joseph Smith, was blessed not only with a great father, but also with a superb mother, Lucy Mack, who influenced a whole dispensation."[11]

Our Heavenly Father has roles for all of his children who will step forward, whether Latter-day Saint or not, whether male or female. Poet and literary critic James Russell Lowell held this belief and expressed it by saying, "No man is ever born into the world whose work is not born with him. Everyone has a job to be done which he is supposed to do and which he can do better than anyone else in the world."[12]

## HELP WANTED

Occasionally "help wanted" signs hang in the windows of businesses. Imagine for a moment that you see another kind of "help wanted" sign. This sign is unique because it has your name on it. This job is for only you because you possess the special talents, gifts, and strengths needed. The sign advertises an opening for you to accept your life mission. What does it say? Only you can discover the answer to that question, and you must look closely or you will miss the sign.

Many people have seen their unique "help wanted" signs throughout history and have taken the jobs. Some see them early on and some see them later in life. It is not so much a matter of your age when you see the sign as long as you recognize the sign with your name on it and take it down from the window to signify that the position has been filled.

Thomas Jefferson saw a sign that said, "Someone needed to write the Declaration of Independence." He saw his name was on it, so he took it down. George Washington saw one that said, "Someone needed to be the father of a remarkable experiment in democracy." He stepped up and took down the sign with his name on it. Abraham Lincoln's help wanted sign said, "Someone needed to save the nation from being torn in two." He stepped forward and took it down.

The young man born February 11, 1847, in Milam, Ohio, was not expendable in the grand scheme of things. Thomas Alva Edison moved to New York City at age twenty-two. About this time, he saw a help wanted sign that read: "Someone needed to be the greatest inventor in history." He soon invented an electric vote recorder. At age thirty, he invented the phonograph. At age thirty-one he invented the electric light bulb and formed a little company called General Electric, which is now one of the largest corporations in the world. He went on to invent the motion picture camera and held a total of 1,093 patents. Edison's help wanted sign is summed up in his philosophy of life: "I never perfected an invention that I did not think about in terms of the service it might give others. I find out what the world needs, then I proceed to invent."

Many people are under the false assumption that this life has no meaning or purpose. They believe that there is nothing they can do that really matters, and that they are only random bits of consciousness. Nothing could be further from the truth. Elder Theodore M. Burton once said, "According to the plan of salvation you were reserved or held back in the heavens as special spirit children to be born in a time and at a place where you could perform a special mission in life. This concept of being foreordained for a special mission is not new. It is referred to many times in the scriptures."[13] The Lord is aware of us and will reveal the part we are to play in mortality if we ask him, and then look for the signs. Surely one of the great sins of life would be to return to God having not discovered or accomplished what we set out in the premortal existence to do.

We have been saved to come to earth at this time for a reason. President Ezra Taft Benson taught:

"For nearly six thousand years, God has held you in reserve to make your appearance in the final days before the Second Coming. Every previous gospel dispensation has drifted into apostasy, but ours will not. . . . God has saved for the final inning some of his strongest children, who will help bear off the kingdom triumphantly. And that is where you come in, for you are the generation that must be prepared to meet your God. . . . Make no mistake about it—you are a marked generation. There has never been more expected of the faithful in such a short period of time as there is of us. . . . Each day we personally make many decisions that show where our support will go. The final outcome is certain—the forces of righteousness will win. What remains to be seen is where each of us personally, now and in the future, will stand in this fight—and how tall we will stand. *Will we be true to our last-days, foreordained mission?*"[14]

## Notes

1. Daniel H. Ludlow, *Encyclopedia of Mormonism*, 521.
2. Neal A. Maxwell, *Things as They Really Are*, 24.
3. "I Am a Child of God," *Hymns*, no. 301.
4. Bruce R. McConkie, *Mormon Doctrine*, 290.
5. Ezra Taft Benson, "To the Young Women of the Church," *Ensign*, November 1986, 81.
6. Joseph B. Wirthlin, *Finding Peace in Our Lives*, 222.
7. Joseph Smith, *History of the Church*, 2:443.
8. Ibid., 6:364, emphasis added.
9. Spencer W. Kimball, "The Role of Righteous Women," *Ensign*, November 1979, 102.
10. Julie B. Beck, "What Latter-day Saint Women Do Best: Stand Strong and Immovable," *Ensign*, November 2007, 110.
11. Neal A. Maxwell, "The Women of God," *Ensign*, May 1978, 10.
12. Sterling W. Sill, *Leadership*, 38.
13. Theodore M. Burton, "Salvation for the Dead—A Missionary Activity," *Ensign*, May 1975, 69.
14. Ezra Taft Benson, "In His Steps," Church Educational System Devotional, Anaheim, California, February 8, 1987, emphasis added.

# CHAPTER 2

~~~

# YOUR PATRIARCHAL BLESSING IS YOUR PERSONAL LIAHONA

*Every worthy member of the Church is entitled to receive*
*such a precious and priceless personal treasure.*

—President Thomas S. Monson

One of the remarkable devices of our day is the Global Positioning System (GPS). This network of twenty-four satellites, placed in orbit by the U.S. Department of Defense, powers a navigation system that, with a hand-held device, can pinpoint exactly where you are and give directions to any destination you choose. It works in any weather condition, anywhere in the world, around the clock. Anyone who has ever been lost can appreciate the benefits of owning one of these devices.

Lehi and his family in a harsh Middle Eastern wilderness used the first known hand-held navigation system. Called the Liahona, it pointed the way the family should go as they walked through miles of desert wasteland. However, it was different from the GPS system of our day in that it only worked if Lehi's family kept God's commandments. When they obeyed, the Liahona guided them to the place that God wanted them to go.

Imagine having the Lord tell you the way to reach the destination he has assigned you. You would never be lost in any weather condition, anywhere in the world, twenty-four hours a day. You can have that device. President Thomas S. Monson shared this insight: "The same

Lord who provided a Liahona to Lehi provides for you and for me today a rare and valuable gift to give direction to our lives, to mark the hazards to our safety, and to chart the way, even safe passage—not to a promised land, but to our heavenly home. The gift to which I refer is known as your patriarchal blessing. Every worthy member of the Church is entitled to receive such a precious and priceless personal treasure."[1]

A Young Women's leader who had counseled girls as they prepared to leave for college told me she had urged them to rely on their patriarchal blessings. She was surprised that only fifteen percent of the young women in her group had received their blessings. Many of the girls were daughters of Church leaders in her area. Later, I mentioned this to a group of priesthood leaders, and one said that he himself had a twenty-three-year-old and a nineteen-year-old who had never received their patriarchal blessings. Without such inspiration, young people are handicapped in their search to define their missions in life.

Several years ago, I was teaching an institute class when two young adults walked in. I had never seen either of them in class before. They introduced themselves as Donald and Monica, both University of Texas students. Throughout the class period, I noticed that Monica looked happy. She kept a big smile on her face the entire hour. I found out after class that she was not a member of the Church. From that point on she began to attend class regularly, and I was able to hear her story.

The weekend before she showed up in my class for the first time, Monica's family had attended a family reunion in south Texas. Her father was a little concerned about her driving there by herself, and so he asked Monica to invite someone to travel with her. She asked Donald, a Latter-day Saint classmate, if he would be willing to drive with her to the reunion, and he agreed. On Sunday morning, during the reunion weekend, Donald decided he should go to church. He looked in the phone book and found a small branch that was quite a distance away. His only clothes were blue jeans, a t-shirt, and flip-flops, but that didn't deter him. Monica felt guilty having him go alone, since she was the one who had asked him to come to her reunion, so she decided to attend his church, too. She borrowed a tank top and a mini-skirt from her aunt and off they went. When the couple walked into the branch meeting, they were treated like royalty. If the branch members noticed their casual dress, no one mentioned it. The Relief Society president paid special attention to Monica. This nineteen-year-old felt something special that day, but also felt unsettled in her beliefs. She went home and recorded this in her journal:

**July 28, 1999:** I feel lost! I am constantly searching for answers, the truth and something to believe in with all of my heart and all of my soul. Throughout my life I have put stock in so many things, not really knowing what it is that I truly believe in or who I really am. I feel now that I am on the threshold of finding what I have been eternally searching for. I believe I will find it in something I have been blind to for all these years— religion. I know that the universe is perfect and it brings at the appropriate time all things that should be. This quest for what is right and something to believe in has always been within me. It is a challenge that I now choose to accept, and I am so grateful to you, God, for presenting me with the challenge. I have always struggled with wanting so many things in life but not always stepping up to the challenge presented before me. I realize that this will not be easy and the answers will not come right away. God, please give me the strength and most of all the courage to continue even when times get hard and the end doesn't even seem in sight. I am making a vow to you and to myself now in this moment that I will not quit and I will not give up just because I think that I cannot do it. I humble myself to you, Lord, so that I may continue to learn from those you have put in my life, but at the same time think enough in myself that I will not be tripped up by the beliefs of others. I accept the challenge!

Monica was soon baptized and jumped enthusiastically into activity in the Church. I remember how excited she was to receive her patriarchal blessing. I counseled her to read the Book of Mormon from cover to cover before she went to the patriarch. She realized, as much as anyone I have ever known, the importance of her blessing and approached it with fasting and prayer. She understood the words of the First Presidency: "Patriarchal blessings contemplate an inspired declaration of the lineage of the recipient and, when so moved upon by the Spirit, an inspired and *prophetic statement of the life mission of the recipient*, together with such blessings, cautions and admonitions as the patriarch may be prompted to give *for the accomplishment of such life mission*."[2]

Monica asked my wife and me to come with her when she received her patriarchal blessing. On the way to the home of the patriarch, Monica confided that she had been fasting and praying that he would answer some very specific questions she had. I worried a little that he would not mention what she desired to know and that perhaps he might even declare her lineage to be from a different tribe than what she expected. That night I gained a stronger testimony of patriarchs and their inspired roles. When the patriarch uttered the words, "You are of the tribe of Judah," chills went up and down my spine, because Monica is a Jewish convert. Both her mother and father are Jewish as were her ancestors. In her first journal entry after visiting that branch meeting, her prayers for strength and courage had been a realization of what it would take to walk away from her religious heritage and traditions.

The blessing was long and beautiful, and the Spirit in the room was strong. Tears streamed down Monica's face as the patriarch spoke. As the blessing appeared to be coming to a close, I was aware that he had not answered all of the questions that she had prayed about. Then the patriarch paused for a long time. When he resumed speaking, he gave her the answers she had prayed for. That night I gained a stronger testimony that the Lord really does know us as individuals. Monica has allowed me to use three more of her journal excerpts to illustrate that principle:

> **March 29, 2000:** What an amazing day! I finished the Book of Mormon for the first time all the way through. Wow! I can say nothing but that I feel like a new person. Faith, hope, and love. That is the secret to life. I have never been happier. I am so lucky and so blessed. Some people spend their whole lives searching for truth and meaning and here I am, twenty years old, and I found it. I was supposed to get my patriarchal blessing today but there was a misunderstanding about the appointment. Fasting and reading the Book of Mormon all day was such an amazing experience. Even though I thought I was prepared, I know that extra week I have will give me an opportunity to learn so much

more and really think about the questions I have about my life."

**April 5, 2000 (Morning):** Today is the day! I am going tonight to get my patriarchal blessing. I can't really explain the feelings I'm having. It's kind of like excitement and nervous anticipation. I have so many questions. Most of them have to *do with my family and future. I am so curious to know if I really am from the tribe of Judah.* I have been thinking of the past so much today and how it relates to my future. I am so grateful for my testimony of the Savior. Last night as I prepared I read more about his atoning sacrifice and his example of perfect love while on this earth. I want so much to emulate that perfect love in my home. I hope tonight that I will learn how to use my God-given gifts to serve the Lord. I have fasted and prayed to *know his will for me,* and I know his servant will reveal it to me. I pray I always will be able to live worthy of the blessings and have the Spirit with me. I dream of the day when *I will stand before God with my husband and he will embrace me and be able to say, "I am proud of you."*

**April 5, 2000 (Night):** It was amazing! I was speechless, breathless! I don't even know what to think. I know with an absolute surety that Patriarch Williams was acting as the voice of the Lord. All the answers to all of my questions were in that blessing. I can't wait to get a copy of it so I can read it over and over and over again. . . . *He said that my husband and I would be able to stand together at the judgment bar and Heavenly Father would be pleased.* At the very end he *talked about my children.* He talked about my talents and said I could use them to lift people up and that *I have a lot of work to do with genealogy. I am from the tribe of Judah*, and he said I would be a *great example* to all those around me. Most important, I learned that Heavenly Father loves me so very much. I have been blessed with so much. I pray that I will be worthy of these amazing blessings and that I won't let my Heavenly Father down. He is the source of all that is good. . . . Any fear of the future has left me and I look forward with faith and anticipation.

Elder LeGrand Richards once said, "When I think of the information that comes to us individually as Latter-day Saints through the patriarchs of this Church, . . . I realize that in the sight of the Almighty we are in very deed individuals, each one with a destiny and a purpose and a mission in life to fill, and I can think of no greater disappointment that could come to one of our Father's children than to finish this life and then be told that he had failed to accomplish the things for which he was sent into this world."[3]

Although it is not common practice to read the patriarchal blessings of others, I have included portions from the blessings of some of our leaders. Here are three from the family of President Gordon B. Hinckley.

> **Blessing to Ada Bittner Hinckley:** "The eye of the Lord has been upon thee from thy birth and a decree of the Father has gone forth that thou *shalt have a mission to fill,* a work to do. . . . Thy name shall be perpetuated and live in the memory of the Saints."[4]

> **Blessing to Bryant S. Hinckley:** "You shall not only become great yourself but your posterity will become great, from your loins shall come forth statesmen, prophets, priests and Kings to the most High God. The Priesthood will never depart from your family, no never. To your posterity there shall be no end . . . and *the name of Hinckley shall be honored in every nation under heaven.*"[5]

> **Blessing to Gordon B. Hinckley:** "Thou shalt grow to the full stature of manhood and shall become a mighty and valiant leader in the midst of Israel. . . . Thou shalt ever be a messenger of peace; the nations of *the earth shall hear thy voice and be brought to a knowledge of the truth by the wonderful testimony which thou shalt bear.*"[6]

You may say, "Well, of course the *Hinckley* family has life missions to perform. But I'm just a common, every day person." An experience recorded by my wife Wendy will shed some light on this thinking:

> When I was in the eighth grade, our English teacher, Mr. Duncan, introduced the class to the fascinating subject of family history. Through his assignment, I became acquainted with several of my ancestors, some of whom gave up much for religious

freedom. My tenth great-grandfather, William Bradford, became the governor of Plymouth colony after making the journey across the Atlantic on the Mayflower. At least two of his descendants became Methodist ministers, the same faith my parents chose to follow. Consequently I had been raised in a good churchgoing home, but we lacked the truths that bring full understanding.

During my teens, I had the opportunity to hear the gospel message, first from Latter-day Saint friends and then from the missionaries. During the missionary discussions, the concept that immediately caught my attention was that of eternal families. Was it really possible to again see my ancestors whom I'd grown to admire so much and my grandfathers who had died when I was young? I began to soak up the gospel truths taught to me. I was baptized, and soon after I received my patriarchal blessing. I was told that I had come through a noble lineage and that I should seek out my kindred dead. From these inspired words, I began to realize how important family history would become in my life.

Before I was married, I gathered the bits of information that my parents had obtained from other relatives. I planned to jump right into searching for ancestors further back on our pedigree, but as is so often the case, my time got filled with other things, some important, some trivial. My ancestors were set on the shelf as I attended college and became engrossed in homemaking and impending motherhood.

Sometimes, though, our anxious ancestors are allowed to give us a swift kick to bring us back to the important matters of life. One night as I slept, I had a dream so real that to this day I can remember vivid details. My husband, Randal, and I were living in a small basement apartment in Provo, Utah, while we attended Brigham Young University. During the night, I suddenly awoke. I opened the bedroom door and, to my utter surprise and delight, found my Grandpa Bradford sitting on the old, ugly turquoise couch in our living room.

I was thirteen when Grandpa died. We had been very close friends, and I admired and loved him greatly. His passing left a huge void in my life, one that seemed to get bigger instead of diminishing over time. Whenever I thought about Grandpa I'd envision him floating in complete darkness with a sad look on his face. An intense fear of death enveloped me after his passing. I had never attended a funeral or seen a person who had passed away, and the thought of doing so brought a dread that was sometimes hard to shake. Even though my fears should have been squelched by the understanding I gained from gospel principles, such as life after death and the resurrection, these fears were deeply embedded and it was hard to fully grasp that these truths applied to me and my family.

Until I found my grandfather sitting on our couch! My previous fear of death was not present at all. It didn't seem strange to have Grandpa sitting there looking up at me. I wanted to run and throw my arms around him. I had missed him so much! But the look on his face made me stop quickly. It was apparent that he had been allowed to come for a specific reason. As I studied his face, I noticed that same sad look that had plagued my thoughts and dreams of the past.

Grandpa looked straight into my eyes and asked, "Why haven't you done my temple work?" I stood dumbfounded with a deep sense of guilt flowing over me, and I was unable to reply. Again he asked: "Wendy, why haven't you done my temple work? Don't you realize that there are many, many people depending on you? You are the only person in the family who can help us!" The full impact of my responsibility as the only member of the Church in my family hit me, and I finally answered, "I will, Grandpa, I will!"

The next morning I awoke feeling wonder about the event that had taken place the night before. I knew for a certainty that my grandfather had accepted the gospel truths in the spirit world but he was unable to receive the needed ordinances there. A great desire welled up inside me to gather the necessary information so the saving ordinances could be performed for him and other relatives who were waiting.

When my husband and I walked into the baptistry at the Provo Temple a few weeks later, we immediately sensed an immense feeling of anticipation and joy. We knew that Grandpa was near and that the joy we felt was radiating from him and his sincere desire to be baptized. Randal was lowered into the waters of the baptismal font as Grandpa's proxy. We again experienced this happy feeling during the endowment session, and later when Grandpa was sealed by proxy to his parents, along with his brothers and sisters.

Since that time, I have conducted much research for these family members of the past. Not only have the necessary names, dates, and places been found, but the actual historical and biographical information has also been gathered, making these people even more real and special to me. They have become my friends.[7]

My wife was drawn to family history in the eighth grade and later it was the same topic that led to her baptism. Her patriarchal blessing counseled her to seek after her family genealogy. She had ignored that counsel, so her grandfather came to her in a vivid dream to wake her up to what her blessing had told her to do. She has since earned a degree in family history from Brigham Young University. Besides being a wife, mother, and grandmother, Wendy's mission in life is to help redeem the dead. She has submitted thousands of names to the temple and helped countless others do the same. She never tires of this work, because she knows that it is one of the duties expected of her when she came to earth. Wendy is just an ordinary member of the Church who followed the counsel of her patriarchal blessing. In the process, she discovered her great mission in life.

Breaking down your patriarchal blessing into specific categories can bring greater understanding and open your eyes to hidden meanings:

- What gifts and talents are mentioned?
- What opportunities will you have in this life?
- What blessings will you receive?
- What counsel and teachings does your blessing give you?
- What insights are given concerning your life mission?

Many have found it helpful to make a reduced copy of their blessing and keep it in their scriptures or planners for easy reference. This provides a constant reminder of what we were sent to earth to accomplish. Patriarchal blessings could be a part of what Isaiah meant when he said, "And thine ears shall hear a word behind thee, saying, this is the way, walk ye in it" (Isaiah 30:21).

President Thomas S. Monson gave this counsel: "Your blessing is not to be folded neatly and tucked away. It is not to be framed or published. Rather, it is to be read. It is to be loved. It is to be followed.

Your patriarchal blessing will see you through the darkest night. It will guide you through life's dangers. Unlike the struggling bomber of yesteryear, lost in the desert wastes, the sands and storms of life will not destroy you on your eternal flight. Your patriarchal blessing is to you a personal Liahona to chart your course and guide your way."[8]

---

## Notes

1. Thomas S. Monson, "A Provident Plan—A Precious Promise," *Ensign*, November 1986, 65.
2. The First Presidency in a letter to stake presidents, June 28, 1958 (emphasis added), as quoted by Thomas S. Monson, "Your Patriarchal Blessing: A Liahona of Light," *Ensign*, November 1986, 65.
3. LeGrand Richards, "Joy in Missionary Work," in Conference Report, April 1946, 84.
4. Sheri L. Dew, *Go Forward with Faith: The Biography of Gordon B. Hinckley*, 20–21 (patriarchal blessing given by John Smith to Ada Bitner, February 1901), emphasis added.
5. Ibid., 22 (patriarchal blessing given by John Ashman, August 8, 1895), emphasis added.
6. Ibid., 60 (received at age eleven from Patriarch Thomas E. Callister), emphasis added.
7. Randal A. Wright, ed., *Forever Friends*, 121–24.
8. Monson, "A Provident Plan—A Precious Promise," 65.

# CHAPTER 3

⚬⚬⚬

# ASK THE LORD SPECIFIC QUESTIONS AND THEN WRITE THE ANSWERS

*You can make every decision in your life correctly if you*
*learn to follow the guidance of the Holy Spirit.*
—Marion G. Romney

The morning after our youngest daughter was married in 2004, my wife and I flew to Georgia to direct a session of Especially for Youth. It was a very busy week, and we had little time to think about the fact that we would be coming home to an empty nest. Before our return flight, we attended an endowment session in the Atlanta Temple. Sitting in the temple, I thought how different life was going to be with no children at home, and I wondered what we were to do. While praying for help, I asked the Lord a specific question: What do you want my wife and me to do now that we will have more free time? I knew my patriarchal blessing referenced traveling in helping to build up the Lord's Kingdom. I reflected on the many places I had already visited in my work for the Church Educational System (CES). Because of family obligations, my wife had only traveled to a few of those places.

Leaving the temple that day, I asked Wendy, "What are we going to do now?" She knew exactly what I was talking about. Not, "What are we going to do right this minute?" but, "What are we going to do now that we are not required to be at the crossroads of our children's lives?" A sudden idea popped into my head: *Why don't we attend an endowment session in every temple in the United States?* We both felt the Lord was involved in that thought. When I got home I wrote down the answer to my prayer: Go to every temple within the United States. We fulfilled that goal when we visited the last dedicated temple in Kona, Hawaii, for our thirty-fifth wedding anniversary in 2007.

What does that have to do with my life mission? It is significant that we visited many of those temples while I was on speaking assignments for CES. While we were in many states, my wife was often able to do family history work. Looking back, the blessings of that revelation have been incredible. Along with traveling to the many temples throughout the United States, we have accomplished the following things:

- Fulfilled the counsel of my patriarchal blessing to travel and help build the kingdom
- Fulfilled the counsel of my wife's patriarchal blessing regarding family history
- Experienced our wonderful nation and its cities and developed a love for all of America
- Revisited important Church history sites, such as Nauvoo, Palmyra, and Kirtland
- Focused on the temple, which is the model for our own homes
- Kept a current temple recommend, a symbol of Church membership and worthiness
- Visited the Orlando temple and, as a sidelight, Disneyworld
- Grew closer in our marriage
- Offered ancestors saving ordinances through temple work

Many blessings occurred because we asked the Lord what we were to do with the next phase of our lives. We will continue to visit new temples as they are dedicated.

Saul asked the Lord a specific question after his life-changing experience on the road to Damascus: "And he trembling and astonished said, Lord, *what wilt thou have me to do?*" (Acts 9:6, emphasis added) Saul was basically asking the Lord what his mission in life should be from that point on. It was a specific question, and the Lord gave him a direct answer. He told him to "Go into the city, and it shall be told thee what thou must do" (Acts 9:6). Saul followed the counsel of the Lord and traveled to Damascus where he was baptized, became known as Paul, and went on to become one of the greatest missionaries of all time. Paul asked a specific question and learned his life mission as a result of that question.

## Benefits of Asking God Questions

There are at least two people who know what your mission is. One of them—you—forgot most of the details upon leaving the premortal existence, so that leaves only one who knows the full scope of things—Heavenly Father. If he sent you to earth with a specific mission to perform, don't you think he would be eager to tell you what it was? You need to "ask in faith, nothing wavering" (James 1:6).

There is power in asking the Lord questions. Joseph Smith was confused about religion and pondered in his heart which church to join. Inspired by a Bible verse, he opened himself to the Spirit, which whispered to him to go to a grove of trees near his home and pray. That prayer led to the First Vision, where God the Father and Jesus Christ appeared to Joseph. He then asked the question on his mind, "[W]hich of all the sects was right?" (*Joseph Smith History* 1:18). The answer he received changed the course of history; he was told to join none of them. That day was also the beginning of Joseph's learning in a line-upon-line process what his mission would be. He was to be the prophet of the last dispensation before the second coming of Christ.

Time passed after this vision, and Joseph said he fell into "many foolish errors" (*Joseph Smith History* 1:28) and often felt condemned by God because of his mistakes. He decided to pray and ask for forgiveness. As before, he approached the Lord with another specific question. This time there was no visit from the Father and Son. Instead, a messenger named Moroni appeared at his bedside and revealed another piece of Joseph's mission. Moroni told him that his name "should be had for good and evil among all nations, kindreds, and tongues, or that it should be both good and evil spoken of among all people" (*Joseph Smith History* 1:33).

Joseph learned a critical lesson. The Lord would answer his specific questions if Joseph went to him in faith. From these experiences and others, we see that Joseph established a pattern of going to the Lord with specific questions to get specific answers. Not only was his personal mission revealed to him, but also many of the doctrines that bring such peace to the members of the restored Church. For example, while working on his translation of the Bible, Joseph came to John 5:29 and had a question: Is there really just one heaven and one hell? The answer became Doctrine and Covenants 76, which revealed the doctrine of the degrees of glory.

Joseph asked the Lord questions throughout his life. Sometimes they related to his personal mission, and sometimes he asked about the missions of others. Several early sections of the Doctrine and Covenants came in answer to questions Joseph asked on behalf of others wanting to know their part in the latter-day restoration. Here are a few examples.

**Hyrum Smith:** "Behold, this is your work, to keep my commandments, yea, with all your might, mind and strength" (Doctrine and Covenants 11:20).

**Joseph Knight:** "Now, as you have asked, behold I say unto you, keep my commandments, and seek to bring forth and establish the cause of Zion" (Doctrine and Covenants 12:6).

**David Whitmer:** "And behold, thou art David, and thou art called to assist; which thing if ye do, and are faithful, ye shall be blessed both spiritually and temporally, and great shall be your reward. Amen" (Doctrine and Covenants 14:11).

**Samuel Smith:** "Behold, I speak a few words unto you, Samuel; for thou also art under no condemnation and thy calling is to exhortation, and to strengthen the church" (Doctrine and Covenants 23:4).

**Emma Smith:** "And the office of thy calling shall be for a comfort unto my servant, Joseph Smith, Jun., thy husband in his afflictions, with consoling words, in the spirit of meekness" (Doctrine and Covenants 25:5).

In addition to asking the Lord specific questions about his life's work, Joseph also was taught to record the answers he received. He was warned of the consequences for not recording revelations received. He said, "For neglecting to write these things when God had revealed them, not esteeming them of sufficient worth, the Spirit may withdraw, and God may be angry; and there is, or was, a vast knowledge, of infinite importance, which is now lost."[1]

## SOME ASPECTS MAY BE DIFFICULT

Not all aspects of our mission will be as adventurous and rewarding as visiting all of the temples. Some things we will be asked to do will be difficult.

Several years ago I had the responsibility to call a returned missionary named Jeremy to an important Church position in which he would be the leader of several people. As we discussed his stewardship, I asked him what his feelings were and if he could accept the calling. He told me that he didn't feel comfortable with the call. While on his mission, he had learned what the Spirit felt like when something was right—peace, joy, warmth, and comfort—and he wasn't feeling any of that about the proposed calling. I told him that I did not want him to accept any assignment that he did not feel comfortable with, and I suggested he go home and think about it.

During the week I saw him at a wedding reception where he informed me that he still did not feel good about accepting the call. I asked him to come to my office a few days later and we would talk about it. When he came in, we reviewed what his duties would entail, and he again expressed conflicted feelings about the calling. He still wasn't feeling the peace and comfort from the Spirit that he had learned to expect while on his mission.

I was about to tell him that I understood and that it would be okay if he did not accept the call. Then words popped into my mind and out of my mouth: "Jeremy, you obviously don't fully understand how the Spirit works, do you?" He looked a little taken aback. I had no idea what I was going to say next, but my words came spilling out. I explained that sometimes when the Spirit speaks to us, we feel peace, joy, and comfort. Other times, however, we feel scared, lonely, and in turmoil. I had never thought of such a thing before.

We then turned to 1 Nephi in the Book of Mormon. I asked him if he thought the Holy Ghost was leading Nephi to get the brass plates which were in the possession of Laban, who was not about to give them up without a fight. Jeremy agreed that the Holy Ghost was prodding Nephi. I then asked if Nephi was feeling peace, joy, warmth, and comfort when the Spirit had to tell him three times to slay Laban. If Nephi was having warm, fuzzy feelings, why did he say, "And I shrunk and would that I might not slay him?" (1 Nephi 4:10.) Nephi was horrified at the prospect of having to kill his kinsman, but he had to have the plates so he could fulfill a portion of his life mission—a mission that he did not fully understand at that point.

Then I asked Jeremy if he thought Heber C. Kimball and Brigham Young were filled with joy to leave their sick families for two to three years because the Spirit whispered they should go afar to preach the gospel. Heber described the scene:

> It was with difficulty we got into the wagon, and started down the hill about ten rods; it appeared to me as though my very inmost parts would melt within me at leaving my family in such a condition, as it were almost in the arms of death. I felt as though I could not endure it. I asked the teamster to stop, and said to Brother Brigham, "This is pretty tough, isn't it; let's rise up and give them a cheer." We arose, and swinging our hats three times over our heads, shouted: "Hurrah, hurrah for Israel." Vilate, hearing the noise, arose from her bed and came to the door. She had a smile on her face. Vilate and Mary Ann Young cried out to us: "Goodbye, God bless you!" We returned the compliment, and then told the driver to go ahead.[2]

Jeremy and I also discussed Spencer W. Kimball's experience when he was called as an Apostle. He recorded his torment in his journal: "My weakness overcame me again. Hot tears came flooding down my cheeks as I made no effort to mop them up. I was accusing myself, and condemning myself and upbraiding myself. I was praying aloud for special blessings from the Lord. I was telling Him that I had not asked for this position, that I was incapable of doing the work, that I was imperfect and weak and human, that I was unworthy of so noble a calling."[3]

That night Jeremy and I learned a valuable lesson about our individual missions; some of the things expected of us may become our passion, while others may fill us with dread. The question is not whether we feel warm and peaceful when the Spirit whispers what we are to do. The question is whether we will do it. I have never met a stake president, bishop, or Relief Society president who jumped up and down with excitement when they were called. Most felt stunned, humbled, overwhelmed and unqualified. But most also knew that it was right and that they needed to accept the call to fulfill the mission to which they had been foreordained.

Often, by accepting opportunities as they are presented to us, we gain the experience needed to move on to the next adventure. Jeremy accepted the call that night and did a wonderful job.

## The Lord Reveals Things Over Time

Even though most of us want to know everything at once, the Lord doesn't quench our thirst with a fire hose. He reveals things to us over time. Even Jesus Christ "received not of the fullness at first, but continued from grace to grace, until he received a fullness" (Doctrine and Covenants 93:13).

Joseph Smith did not learn the full extent of his mission at first. Even when he asked specific questions, the answers were usually revealed over time. For example, he had a legitimate question about where to build the latter-day city of Zion. Look how the Lord responded concerning this critical topic. Notice also that Joseph made sure these important answers were recorded:

> **September 1830:** "Behold, I say unto you that it shall be on the borders by the Lamanites." (Doctrine and Covenants 28:9)
> **June 1831:** "[I]f ye are faithful ye shall assemble yourselves together to rejoice upon the land of Missouri, which is the land of your inheritance, which is now the land of your enemies." (Doctrine and Covenants 52:42)
> **July 1831:** "Behold, the place which is now called Independence is the center place; and a spot for the temple is lying westward, upon a lot which is not far from the courthouse." (Doctrine and Covenants 57:3).]

Over a ten-month period Joseph first learned that the center place of Zion would be somewhere on the borders by the Lamanites—the vast American frontier. He next learned that it would be in the land of Missouri. He finally learned that Zion would be in the city of Independence and even the exact spot designated for the temple there.

Nephi didn't know his entire life mission at first, beginning with the task of getting the brass plates. He gave valuable insight about the process the Lord used with him when he said, "And I was led by the Spirit, not knowing beforehand the things which I should do" (1 Nephi 4:6). Because of Nephi's obedience, the Lord revealed to him the step-by-step plan to accomplish that first assignment.

The Lord does the same thing regarding his will for us. It may take days, months, or even years to see our life mission unfold. But if we go in faith, asking the Lord specific questions along the way, he will give us the answers and show us the way. When we receive these answers, we must record them for clarity and remembrance.

## ASK QUESTIONS AND PONDER

Do you ask the Lord specific questions about his will for you? Do you write down the answers you receive? Always remember that there never was a revelation without a question being asked first. Part of the revelation process is to ponder what it is you are to do. President Spencer W. Kimball said, "I am hopeful that each of you will ponder carefully what it is the Lord would have you do with your lives, with the special skills, training, and testimonies you have."[4]

I challenge you to write down the following question: *What mission was I sent to earth to perform?* Then over the course of days, weeks, months, and even years record the promptings that come to you when you ponder the question and listen for answers. President Ezra Taft Benson spoke about this process when he said, "Do you take time to listen to the promptings of the Spirit? Answers to prayer come most often by a still voice and are discerned by our deepest, innermost feelings. I tell you that you can know the will of God concerning yourselves if you will take the time to pray and to listen."[5]

When I was young, my parents owned a grocery store. One day my dad's sister-in-law came by with her young daughter Brenda. My cousin looked at the candy counter and pointed to several candy bars she wanted. Each time she asked for a specific brand, her mother would say, "Oh, you don't want that." Finally, after pointing to about five different candy bars and getting the same response from her mother, the exasperated little girl asked, "Well, what does me want?" You need to ask your Father in Heaven "What is it that I really want?" since he knows the answer to that much better than you do.

Finally, it is critical that you remember that answers will not be revealed unless you are living worthy to receive them. Elder Bruce R. McConkie said, "It is not a call to a special office that opens the windows of revelation to a truth seeker. Rather it is personal righteousness."[6]

## Notes

1. Joseph Fielding Smith, *Teachings of the Prophet Joseph Smith*, 72–73.
2. Orson F. Whitney, *Life of Heber C. Kimball*, 265–66.
3. Edward L. and Andrew E. Kimball Jr., *Spencer W. Kimball: Twelfth President of The Church of Jesus Christ of Latter-day Saints*, 193.
4. Spencer W. and Edward L. Kimball, *Teachings of Spencer W. Kimball*, 440.
5. Ezra Taft Benson, "A Message to the Rising Generation," *Ensign*, November 1977, 30.
6. Bruce R. McConkie, in Conference Report, October 1969, 82.

# CHAPTER 4

⟨✥⟩

# RECOGNIZE AND MAKE USE OF YOUR GIFTS, TALENTS, AND STRENGTHS

*To every man is given a gift by the Spirit of God.*
—Doctrine and Covenants 46:11

In September 1972, my brother Jack and I were at Brigham Young University, keeping an eye on the summer Olympic Games with every expectation that our Texas hometown hero, James Busceme, would pummel his way to a gold medal in boxing. It can be a brutal sport, but we overlooked that in our loyalty to a fellow Texan, a five-time state Golden Gloves boxer and four-time national Golden Gloves champion. As newly minted boxing fans, we closely followed the preliminary events on the news, which is where we learned that our man had lost in the third round to a Polish boxer before we could even see him compete on television. In fact, all the U.S. boxers but one were sent packing that year before reaching the gold medal round.

The only U.S. boxer left in the finals was "Sugar Ray" Seals, a 6-foot-1-inch southpaw from Tacoma, Washington, weighing in at a spindly 139 pounds. The glowering pugilists from the communist bloc nations were dominating boxing that year. In a Cold War move, my brother and I quickly switched our loyalties to Sugar Ray. Before the match, highlights of Ray's opponent named Angel Angelov were shown on TV. He was a classic communist-style boxer from Bulgaria, built like the Incredible Hulk. Angelov had dominated all his previous fights and was heavily favored to win the gold medal.

We had never seen Sugar Ray Seals fight and knew nothing about him. When Jack and I saw how tall and skinny Ray Seals was, we were afraid the Bulgarian boxer would wipe the mat with him. Ray had a very high-pitched voice and sounded like a prepubescent teenager. Before the match, he was interviewed by veteran sportscaster Howard Cosell and asked what he thought his chances were against the Bulgarian. Ray said, "Well, he's good. He's really good! But I think I can beat him with my superior boxing ability." Maybe it was because his voice was so high or because he was so skinny, but when he made that comment, my brother and I laughed out loud. I remember thinking that we wouldn't be hearing "The Star Spangled Banner" on the winner's stand that year.

In the first round, Angelov completely dominated Sugar Ray, just as we had feared. Between rounds, however, something happened. Ray's trainers must have reminded him of the gift he had. It was not bulging muscles like his opponent had. In fact, he appeared to have no muscles to speak of. It turned out that his great gift was in the length of his skinny arms. Round two became a test of brute strength against long arms. Sugar Ray jabbed relentlessly with those long arms and began scoring points. Sitting on the edge of our seats, my brother and I cheered loudly. In the end, Sugar Ray Seals won the only gold medal in boxing for the United States during the 1972 Olympics. It was an unbelievable turn of events, one that shocked even the boxing experts. Ray Seals had used his gift to win against tremendous odds.

Your mission is not so different from the mission of the young boxer. In one corner you have Satan and his forces, the heavy favorites going into the match. They are big, strong, and intimidating. They have an unparalleled winning streak and have destroyed the life missions of countless millions. In the other corner is the skinny little opponent, a mirror of you. The world, and perhaps even a few friends, urge you to throw in the towel, because there is no way you can win against such odds. But you courageously continue on with your mission. The first round doesn't look good because of the many mistakes you make—you are getting beaten up. But between rounds, your trainer whispers something in your ear: You have a gift that will help you go the distance against the adversary. What is this gift? That is for you to hear from your trainer. But if you don't, you will find yourself flat on the mat while the adversary punches the air in a victory dance above you.

I love to see someone win against tremendous odds. Someone who won his fight and completed his assigned mission was Hyrum Smith. One of his trainers was his father, who revealed to Hyrum his greatest gift in a blessing. Elder M. Russell Ballard, a direct descendant of Hyrum, said, "In September of 1840, Joseph Smith Sr. gathered his family around him. This venerable patriarch was dying and wanted to leave his blessing on his beloved wife and children. Hyrum, the eldest living son, asked his father to intercede with heaven when he arrived there so the enemies of the Church 'may not have so much power' over the Latter-day Saints. Father Smith then laid his hands upon Hyrum's head and blessed him to have 'peace . . . sufficient . . . to accomplish the work which God has given you to do.' Knowing of Hyrum's lifelong faithfulness, he concluded this last blessing with the promise that Hyrum would 'be as firm as the pillars of heaven unto the end of his days.'"[1] This blessing identified Hyrum's strongest characteristic; he was "firm as the pillars of heaven." Throughout Hyrum's life, the forces of evil combined against him in an attempt to defeat him or at least prompt him to stray off course.

Hyrum passed his test and remained as "firm as the pillars of heaven unto the end of his days" and sealed his testimony in blood along with the prophet Joseph Smith. Surely like Hyrum, the Lord has blessed us with gifts to help us win the battle against the forces of evil. "For all have not every gift given unto them; for there are many gifts, and to *every man is given a gift* by the Spirit of God" (Doctrine and Covenants 46:11, emphasis added).

## Natural Gifts and Talents

We all inherit certain gifts, talents, and strengths. Some are easily observable, while others are never seen with the eye but must be discerned by the heart.

Our complex society needs many people's gifts to make it function. One person has a burning desire to be a surgeon, while another fashions the precision surgical tools. Still another is the steady, long haul truck driver who delivers the tools to the hospital where another wipes the fevered brow of the waiting patient. They all work together as if they were part of a divine plan. How is it that so many different aspirations exist within the human species?

Our gifts are revealed to us over the course of our lives. Family members, friends, and our own experiences help solidify this knowledge. As we discover those unique abilities, our God-given gifts and talents can lead to exceptional accomplishments.

How did Michael Jordan get to be one of the greatest basketball players in history? Was it because he worked harder and practiced more than anyone else who ever played the game? Indeed, he worked hard, but others have worked just as hard or even harder. Was it the good coaching he received? Good coaching helps, but everyone else on the team, including those sitting on the bench, got the same coaching. The difference is that Michael Jordan had physical gifts. His size, speed, eye-hand coordination, and jumping ability made him a natural for basketball, and, as he discovered, not for baseball.

Your gifts may not be physical like Michael Jordan's, but you have unique gifts that are just as real, and they are key to the life mission that only you can accomplish. The Lord saved you to come to mortality during this day and time. He gave you the gifts and talents to make it happen. President Wilford Woodruff said, "The Lord has chosen a small number of choice spirits of sons and daughters out of all the creations of God, who are to inherit this earth; and this company of choice spirits have been kept in the spirit world for six thousand years to come forth in the last days to stand in the flesh in this last dispensation of the fullness of times, to organize the kingdom of God upon the earth, to build it up and to defend it and to receive the eternal and everlasting priesthood of God."[2]

# DISCOVER YOUR GREATEST GIFT

Several years ago I spoke at a youth conference in Hillsboro, Oregon. One of the other speakers was Steve James, a popular musician and songwriter. We stayed in the home of Joanna, who was the stake Young Women's president. One night after a dance, Steve and I, along with some of Joanna's teenaged children and several of their friends gathered in their family room. It was late, but they begged to hear Steve play the piano and sing. We were having a great time when one of her children exclaimed, "Hey, Mom wrote a song! You should have her sing it for you!" Joanna turned red and quickly declined the invitation, but we were feeling expansive and encouraged her to sing it for us.

One of her teenagers told us that they had a recording of the song and would play it for us. Joanna didn't like the attention but they played the song anyway. Soon, she was being pressured again to sing it live for us. She explained that she didn't have the sheet music; a friend had borrowed it to work on an arrangement. The teens tried their best to persuade Joanna to call her friend and offered to go pick up the music. Steve and I thought it was a great idea, and we pushed her to make the call. She reminded us that it would be rude to call at that time of night, so we backed off. During this dialogue, Steve told her several times that he would play the song for her if she would sing. Again, she reminded him that she did not have the music and it was too late to get it.

Finally, Steve walked over to the piano and played the song from start to finish from memory. Joanna cried as the rest of us sat in amazement. He had heard the recorded song played *one* time and was then able to recreate it. Someone commented, "You must have practiced a long time to be able to do that." I thought, no, it was a gift. Steve certainly had practiced long and hard, but no amount of practice will allow a person to do what he did that night, absent some innate talent. My wife taught piano for twenty years. She plays well but can't play anything without the music in front of her. She developed a talent; Steve discovered one of his gifts. He then magnified that gift through countless hours of practice. Because of Steve's remarkable musical gift, he has been able to bless the lives of thousands of young people throughout the nation. That gift is helping fulfill the mission he was sent to accomplish.

If you are given gifts or talents that you do not magnify, you will surely be held accountable for that. President Joseph F. Smith said, "Every son and every daughter of God has received some talent, and each will be held to strict account for the use or misuse to which it is put."[3]

Over the years, I have noticed the unique gifts and talents that our prophets have displayed and how they have used them to fulfill their appointed missions. Nephi had a mission to persuade all to come unto Christ. To accomplish that mission he needed to discover his gifts and talents. Nephi had the gift of faith to "go and do" anything the Lord commanded. He personally refined the ore to make metal plates on which he kept his record. He also knew the Hebrew and Egyptian languages and reformed the Egyptian to write upon the plates (1 Nephi 1:2). He made a bow of wood when his steel bow broke (1 Nephi 16:23). He was a skilled hunter who did "slay wild beasts" (1 Nephi 16:31). He fashioned metal tools, to build a ship of "exceeding fine" workmanship (1 Nephi 17:16). He established a city, built a temple, and taught his people to build buildings and to work with gold, silver brass, copper, iron, steel, and wood. Using the sword of Laban for a guide, he made weapons, for the defense of his people (2 Nephi 5:14). All of these things played into his mission.

Joseph Smith became a modern day Nephi and did whatever the Lord commanded him to do. His gifts and talents exceeded that which would have occurred naturally in a nineteenth century farm boy. He was a record keeper, military general, mayor, city builder, scriptorian, linguist, translator of ancient languages, temple builder, Church president, colonizer, and public speaker. Because of his gifts and talents, Joseph was fearless and had no doubt that the Lord would help him succeed in whatever he was asked to do.

The Lord wants you to recognize the tools you have been given to accomplish your mission. Brigham Young said, "Every man and woman who has talent and hides it will be called a slothful servant. Improve day by day upon the capital you have. In proportion as we are capacitated to receive, so it is our duty to do."[4]

Sometimes we spend our time wishing for gifts that we do not have. There are thousands who wish they could sing like Luciano Pavarotti, but they can't. That doesn't mean we shouldn't try to improve that talent. But if singing is not your gift, you probably never will sing like he sings. Your time would be better spent seeking out your own gifts.

When I was young, I was training to be a professional basketball player. I thought that would be my mission in life. I prayed about it a lot and played out my fantasy shooting baskets a couple of times a week at a basketball hoop near the church. I think I could have reached the pros except for these few things that held me back:

- I was small for my age
- I couldn't dribble the ball very well

- My passing was not good
- I couldn't jump very high
- I didn't have a good shot
- I was slow and wasn't very good at defense

Save those shortcomings, you might have read about my NBA career. I could have improved my game with thousands of hours of practice, but I was spending my time in a world of pipe dreams. It had nothing to do with reality or with the gifts and talents I'd been given. It does no good to chase your life mission with dreams of having other people's gifts.

Sometimes we become discouraged as we compare our gifts and talents to those others possess. In 1989, I attended a talent show held at the Especially for Youth program on the Texas A&M University campus. Sitting next to Ron Hills, the founder of the EFY program, I witnessed more amateur talent that night than I'd ever seen on one stage. I leaned over to Ron and said, "Wow, I feel like a nobody right now." He knew exactly what I was talking about. He leaned over to me and said, "Just think, Brother Wright, without a good audience they would be nothing!" I never forgot the lesson he taught me that day. Just because you don't have the same gifts and talents as someone else, it does not mean you need to envy them. There is a time for you to clap and cheer others with different talents. There is no need to compare our weaknesses to others' strengths. One day it will be their turn to cheer for you.

Some find it hard to comprehend that all can be given gifts and talents customized for their mission only. They underestimate the power of our Creator. With a world population of approximately 6.7 billion people, how many of these people look exactly alike? There may be a few who have a similar look, but those who know them can distinguish even identical twins. If every person on earth could be given a different face, then why is it so hard to believe that they have been given different gifts and talents to perform a unique mission?

It is critical that you don't spend time worrying about the abilities of others while neglecting what you have been given. In the parable of the talents, the Savior gave one of his most bitter rebukes to one who buried his talent. "Take therefore the talent from him, and give it to him which hath ten talents" (Matthew 25:28). Because of his fear of what others might do or say concerning the development of his talents, this man chose to bury his God-given endowment. The other servants who increased their talents were blessed with more and received commendation from the Lord: "Well done, thou good and faithful servant" (Matthew 25:21). If the slothful man had worked to improve what the Lord allotted him, without being concerned with the "fear of man" (Doctrine and Covenants 60:2), he would have been offered more talents. Benjamin Franklin echoed this principle when he said, "Hide not your talents, they for use were made. What's a sundial in the shade?"[5]

Over the course of your life, you will find out what you are really good at. Those around you, along with our own experiences, will reveal it to you. Aristotle understood this discovery process when he said, "Where your talents and the needs of the world cross, there lies your vocation."[6] President James E. Faust said, "You cannot imagine the gifts and talents each of you has."[7]

With that in mind, isn't it time that you discovered the gifts and talents that are personally yours? I challenge you to spend a week compiling a written list of your gifts, talents, and strengths. Are there more talents the Lord wants you to use? What might they be and how will you develop them?

Notes

1. Lucy Mack Smith, *History of Joseph Smith*, 309, as quoted by M. Russell Ballard, "Hyrum Smith: 'Firm as the Pillars of Heaven,'" *Ensign*, November 1995, 6.
2. Ezra Taft Benson, *Title of Liberty*, 197.
3. Joseph F. Smith, "The Returned Missionary," *Juvenile Instructor*, November 1903, 689.
4. Brigham Young, *Journal of Discourses*, 7:7.
5. Benjamin Franklin, *Poor Richard's Almanac*, October 1750.
6. Aristotle, wiki.wsmoak.net.
7. James E. Faust, "What It Means to Be a Daughter of God," *Ensign*, November 1999, 100.

# CHAPTER 5

───── ⦿⦿⦿ ─────

# RECOGNIZE AND OVERCOME YOUR WEAKNESSES

*I give unto men weaknesses that they may be humble.*
—Ether 12:27

A petite woman named Goldie Ashcraft taught me a lesson in a testimony meeting in Bay City, Texas. Goldie, who appeared to be in her nineties, was helped to the stand to bear her testimony. Radiating happiness and speaking with her strong southern accent, she began:

> My dad joined the Church in 1890 with one of my brothers and my sister. I joined the Church later when I was eight years old. I never missed a day of church until I got married. One weekend we had visitors come from the eastern U.S. I wanted to show them a good time and take them to do something fun. But, the only day we had to do anything fun was on Sunday. Now, I wanted to take them to the beach in the worst way! I talked to my husband and said, "Let's take them to the beach on Sunday."
> And he said, "Okay."

I was sure Goldie was about to tell us that they all had a miserable time. She would bear testimony of keeping the Sabbath holy, and her story would end. But she continued with a twinkle in her eye:

> We went to the beach that Sunday and missed church to do it. I want you to know we had a glorious time that day! But the

next day I didn't feel so good. Two missionaries came over to visit our home that afternoon. One of them looked at me and said, "Sister Ashcraft, you don't feel so good, do you?"

"No, I don't," I replied.

"You feel like h-e–double hockey sticks, don't you?"

"Yes, I do."

Then the missionary said, "It's because you didn't go to church yesterday."

I said, "Yes, I know."

Then Goldie said something I will never forget: "I want everyone here to know that I have never missed another Sunday since that time!" Although she had given in to a moment of weakness long ago, she had changed and made a commitment never to miss church again. Her weakness had become her strength.

A weakness is defined as an inadequate or defective quality, as in a person's character—a slight fault or defect. You have weaknesses, and overcoming them is key to achieving your life mission.

You are a dual being with a spiritual side and a physical or "natural" side, which some refer to as your "animal side." One of the main purposes of life is to learn to control and put off the tendencies of that natural man. Elder Neal A. Maxwell offered some ways to do this: "I need, for instance, to develop humility and meekness, but the tendency of us mortals is toward pride. We are to develop patience, but the natural man is impatient. We are to be pure, but the natural man tends toward corruption. We are to be spiritually submissive, but the natural man tends toward selfishness and aggressiveness. We are to endure well, but, left to our natural tendencies, we would give up."[1]

Some traditions can have a negative effect on those exposed to them. If these patterns are not changed, they can even destroy the mission a person was sent to accomplish. In the Book of Mormon, Laman was the birthright son and stood to gain half of his father's material possessions, along with the leadership of the clan upon his father's death. But he felt he was wronged by Nephi, who lost much of the family's wealth—Laman's inheritance—when he used it to bargain for the brass plates. When that plan failed and Nephi had to kill Laban to get the plates, it meant the family could never return to

Jerusalem. From Laman's perspective, he had lost his birthright and his home because of Nephi's actions. So, Laman tried to kill Nephi, and that hatred was passed to their descendants. Perhaps millions died in the next thousand years because of the wicked traditions of their fathers. "They [the Lamanites] were a wild, and ferocious, and a blood-thirsty people, believing in the tradition of their fathers, which is this—Believing that they were driven out of the land of Jerusalem because of the iniquities of their fathers, and that they were wronged" (Mosiah 10:12). How many were distracted from their purpose in life because of these traditions, until finally the Nephites were destroyed in the last great battle?

What traditions have been passed to you that may be holding you back? Perhaps you grew up in a home where anger and yelling was part of everyday life. If you are not consciously aware of the impact on you of that negative behavior, you could easily pass on that family "tradition." Brigham Young shared his feelings on the power of traditions in the home: "Whether surrounded with error or truth, the web woven around them in childhood days lasts, and seldom wears threadbare. . . . The traditions of my earliest recollection are so forcible upon me that it seems impossible for me to get rid of them. And so it is with others; hence the necessity of correct training in childhood."[2] Depending on how they are handled, your life experiences can have a major impact on you and potentially lead to weaknesses.

Up until the fifth grade, I was a good student and made better than average grades. Then suddenly my grades dropped dramatically. I was in Mr. Singer's class that year and had a crush on a girl at my school. As I thought about her, I was inspired to write a song. I was sitting in class one day putting the final touches to this song when I should have been paying attention to Mr. Singer. The tune was playing in my head as I polished the lyrics, oblivious to Mr. Singer's lecture. Suddenly, he was beside my desk and, without warning, snatched up my song sheet. He began laughing as he walked to the front and told the class to listen up. He then read my amateurish words to the entire class. They didn't just laugh; they were almost rolling in the aisles, while I slumped in my chair with a crimson face.

That experience had a major impact on my life. I lost respect for and trust in teachers and essentially gave up in school. For the rest of my early public education, I didn't try, and my grades suffered. I became shy and withdrawn. I especially hated to write or speak in front of a group. I had no desire to pursue education past high school. Many years passed before I realized the devastating impact that event had on me. But looking back on this and other setbacks in my life, I can see they were part of the process of discovering and achieving my life mission. They became tests to see if I would let the Lord help me turn my weaknesses into strengths.

It took me years to put those experiences into perspective. That boy who hated school got a PhD, and the lad who distrusted teachers grew up to be one. The child who shrank in humiliation when his words were read aloud in front of his peers now speaks regularly to gatherings of hundreds of teens and young adults. (Somehow, though, I never brought myself to write another song. Apparently that is not one of my gifts.)

Your greatest weaknesses can be turned into your greatest strengths with the Lord's help. "And if men come unto me I will show unto them their weakness. *I give unto men weakness* that they may be humble; and my grace is sufficient for all men that humble themselves before me; for if they humble themselves before me, and have faith in me, then will I make weak things become strong unto them" (Ether 12:27, emphasis added).

When we think of prophets, we generally think of their great work, not their weaknesses. However, even prophets have weaknesses that they must overcome. Consider the weaknesses of three great prophets and how the Lord turned them to strengths.

# PRESIDENT SPENCER W. KIMBALL

President Kimball was a kind, yet powerful, leader. He was also a mortal man with weaknesses. A story from the early years of his marriage demonstrates one of his weaknesses: "There were occasional disagreements, of course. One summer when Camilla wanted to save their extra cash for a new house and Spencer wanted to travel, they simply did not come to agreement. So Spencer loaded the car and took the trip alone and had a good time."[3]

President Kimball thought a nice vacation was the right thing to do with their extra money, while Camilla thought she was right to save for a home. Even though we lack details in this story, we can't help but think that Spencer still had something to learn about compromise at that early stage of his marriage. We all have this "natural" inclination at times. Elder Lynn G. Robbins explains, "The natural man has a tendency to think only of himself."[4]

This situation demonstrates one of President Kimball's early weaknesses. Not many right-thinking husbands would dip into the family's nest egg for a solo vacation. On a positive note, President Kimball was willing to stand up for what he felt strongly about. In time, this soon-to-be prophet was tempered and refined to add kindness, gentleness, and compromise to his strong personality. Thus, throughout his life mission, he repeatedly was willing to stand up for what he believed in. He became a plain spoken and courageous prophet who was also full of empathy. The Lord took the potential weakness of being strong-willed and led Spencer W. Kimball on a life mission that would end up blessing the lives of millions. Consider the influence that his straight-talking book, *The Miracle of Forgiveness*, has had on members of the Church over the years. This book is an example of his plain, but loving, teaching. The Lord took one of President Kimball's weaknesses and turned it into one of his greatest strengths. He can do the same with you.

# PRESIDENT GORDON B. HINCKLEY

See if you can pick out a weakness in the following short examples from a biography of President Hinckley:

- The Hinckley version of a trip to the beach was unorthodox. "When we went to the beach, we went to look, not to play in the sand," Marjorie [his wife] explained. "Five minutes after we were there, Gordon said, Okay, you've seen the ocean. Let's go."[5]

- Efficiency and punctuality were Hinckley trademarks— hence his impatience with anything that infringed on his time, such as crowds and lines. On Memorial Day, the family began their annual pilgrimage to decorate Grandma Bitner's and Aunt May's graves well before 7:00 AM to "beat the crowds." (As adults the children were shocked to find that they could drive right to their grandmother's grave at noon without getting caught in traffic.) By Gordon's definition, half a dozen cars in a given place at any time constituted a crowd.[6]

- Each summer the family went to the drive-in movie at least once, but they literally never saw the end of a show. Before the feature was over, Gordon headed for the exit rather than risk getting penned in by a line of traffic. If a wedding reception started at 6:00 PM, he and Marjorie arrived at 5:30 to avoid the crowd.[7]

President Hinckley struggled with impatience. What did the Lord do with that shortcoming? He turned it into President Hinckley's greatest strength. Consider what he accomplished during his years as president of the Church. At the October 1997 General Conference of the Church, he announced the inspired plan for building small temples. At that time there were fifty-one temples worldwide. Three years later in December 2000, there were 102 dedicated temples. It took from 1836 to 1997 to get our first fifty-one temples and three years to get fifty-one more. That is a miracle. President Gordon B. Hinckley was sent to earth to become the greatest temple builder in world history. The Lord took a weakness and turned it into a strength that blessed the entire world.

## Nephi

Nephi is one of those prophets who appeared to be so righteous that it is hard to imagine that he had any weakness to overcome. And yet he wallowed in a flaw so serious that Christ himself said those who have it are "in danger of the judgment" (see Matthew 5:22). Nephi confessed his weakness to the whole world and described the consequences it had for him. At one point he was so depressed about it that he was ready to give up. Consider the following verses from 2 Nephi 4:

- "O wretched man that I am" (v.17)

- "My heart sorroweth because of my flesh" (v.17)
- "My soul grieveth because of mine iniquities" (v.17)
- "I am encompassed about because of temptations and sins which do so easily beset me" (v.18)
- "My heart groaneth because of my sins" (v.19)

What is that weakness? Nephi is "angry because of mine enemy" (v. 27). Who is this enemy? He names them in verse 22: "He hath confounded mine enemies, unto the causing of them [my brothers] to quake before me." Most of us would say Nephi's anger toward his brothers was justified. They tried to kill him, beat him so badly with a rod that an angel had to intervene, and tied him up on a ship causing great sufferings while his wife and children watched in agony and his parents hovered near death. Yet, Nephi did not give in to his anger until one event that apparently was the straw that broke the camel's back: "And it came to pass that he [Lehi] died, and was buried. And it came to pass that not many days after his death, Laman and Lemuel and the sons of Ishmael were angry with me because of the admonitions of the Lord" (2 Nephi 4:13). When Nephi was mourning the loss of his father, with whom he had shared so many spiritual highs, his brothers continued to provoke him. At that point, Nephi recorded his own descent into anger.

However, with the Lord's help, that anger turned to love. Nephi later said, "For I pray continually for them [his brothers and their families] by day, and mine eyes water my pillow by night, because of them" (2 Nephi 33:3). He taught his people also to love the Lamanites, and his descendents spent nearly a thousand years trying to bring them to Christ.

In the end, one of Nephi's direct descendants said, "Now I, Moroni, write somewhat as seemeth me good; and I write unto my brethren, the Lamanites; and I would that they should know" (Moroni 10:1). Moroni recorded his message for the very people who destroyed his family, friends, and civilization. It is to the Lamanites that Moroni specifically wrote when he gave the great challenge to ask for a witness of the truth of his record, the Book of Mormon (Moroni 10:4–5).

Nephi never blamed anyone else for his weakness (not even his brothers), even though that is the tendency of the natural man. Instead, he wrote, "O wretched man *that I am*! Yea, my heart sorroweth because of *my flesh*; my soul grieveth because of *mine iniquities*" (2 Nephi 4:17 emphasis added). He took responsibility for his own weakness.

# TAKE RESPONSIBILITY

When I was an undergraduate student at BYU, I took an organizational behavior class from Stephen R. Covey. Right before class started one day, a classmate walked to the front and informed the teacher, "Brother Covey, I won't be at class on Friday because I have to go to a tennis tournament in Albuquerque."

Brother Covey replied, "No, you don't have to go, you choose to go."

The student retorted, "No, I'm on the BYU tennis team, and we have matches at the University of New Mexico. I have to go!"

Adamantly, Brother Covey came back, "No, you choose to go."

The student said, "You don't understand."

Brother Covey finally said, "I understand perfectly. You are on the BYU tennis team, and you choose to go to Albuquerque on Friday rather than come to my class."

The student finally agreed, "Okay. I choose to compete in the tournament rather than come to class."

I'll never forget what Brother Covey said next: "I don't blame you at all. That is exactly what I would do, but don't blame your decisions on other factors."

The message is clear. We are free to choose. There is no justification in blaming others.

We all have weaknesses to work on. I became painfully aware of some of mine when my wife and I made lists of our gifts, talents, and strengths, and then our weaknesses. I probed the depths of my soul and came up with three or four things that were holding me back, but I wanted to make sure there were no more. I prayed for the Lord to make others apparent to me during the next twenty-four hour period.

From Saturday, July 15, to Sunday, July 16, 2001, I asked the Lord to help me see my weaknesses. That day I added seventy-five more to the list I thought was complete. On the way to oversee a young adult activity at the Austin, Texas, LDS Institute on Saturday night, I looked at the time and realized I was twenty minutes late (*not punctual*). Then I thought, "Mark my words. There won't be any other adult supervision at the activity besides me" (*martyr*). Sitting in my office at the Institute, I worried about my daughter who was not home from a temple trip to Dallas *(obsessive worrier)*. I was irritated with her because she hadn't called *(temper)*. When I realized that I hadn't mingled with anyone at the activity (*unfriendly),* I left my office and met a young man with a very unusual name and thought, "Who in the world would name their kid that" (*judgmental)*? When I looked down, I noticed a huge tattoo on his leg and wondered why he would do that (*critical)*. I thought, "That's like having a polyester suit from the 70s welded onto your skin for life. When the styles have long since passed, the tattoo remains" (*sarcastic)*. Returning to my office, I looked up scripture references, as well as modern prophets' teachings, and found very little about tattoos, but references about judging were everywhere.

After the activity, I stopped by the grocery store to pick up a few things we needed. At the check out, I noticed it was 12:20 AM (*Sabbath breaker)*. I finally got to bed at 1:00 AM *(not early to bed)*. I had to arise early to drive to San Antonio and was not happy about it (*griper)*. While driving down Interstate 35, I jotted a note in my planner (*distracted driver)*. The note was to remind myself to speak to my wife about her tendency to drive too fast *(mote in neighbor's eye)*. I looked up and saw I was doing seventy-five in a sixty-five mph zone *(law breaker)*.

I was serving in the San Antonio mission presidency at that time, and it was my first meeting with our new mission president. When he wasn't at the appointed meeting place at 8:30 AM, I got a little irritated *(impatient)*. I waited for an hour, which seemed like a sacrifice of pioneer proportions to me (*exaggerator)*. When I got back to Austin, I was ready to tell my wife that our new mission president was a little unreliable. As soon as I walked in the door, Wendy said the mission president had called to ask where I was. "He told you the meeting would be at the mission home, not the mission office" *(not paying attention)*. I had never gone to a meeting there before with the previous mission president; he should have known that *(blame others)*. I went to another ward that met in our building since I missed my own and began to work on a talk I had to give (*discourteous)*. While the congregation sang the opening song, it hit me that I seldom sing the hymns in church (*rebellious*). During the opening prayer, I opened my eyes to see who was praying (*disrespectful*). While the Sacrament was being passed, I thought of things that needed to get done the next day (*irreverent*). During the special musical number, I commented to the boy sitting by me how good the music was (*disruptive*). During one of the talks, I got really sleepy and almost dozed off (*inattentive*). I finally asked the Lord to please slow down the revelation process; I had plenty to work on during my lifetime.

Recognizing your weaknesses can give you motivation to change, but sometimes the revelation can be a source of discouragement. It is one thing to face up to your weaknesses and work on them and another to dwell on them and get discouraged. Don't punish yourself. Discouragement is not the Lord's way; it is Satan's. The devil emphasizes our weaknesses, while the Lord stresses our ability to overcome. Lorenzo Snow once said, "Do not be discouraged. If the Apostle Peter had become discouraged at his manifest failure to maintain the position that he had taken to stand by the Savior under all circumstances, he would have lost all; whereas, by repenting and persevering he lost nothing but gained all, leaving us too to profit by his experience. . . . We must not allow ourselves to be discouraged whenever we discover our weakness."[8]

Satan loves to whisper in your ear that you are weak and worthless and there is no need to try. He will tell you that you can't accomplish your mission. I like what Vincent Van Gogh reportedly said: "If you hear a voice within you say, 'You are not a painter,' then by all means paint . . . and that voice will be silenced."[9] You have been promised that you can shut down the voice of the adversary. "Submit yourselves therefore to God. Resist the devil, and he will flee from you" (James 4:7). Remember that with the Lord's help, you can turn any weakness into strength.

Spend several days prayerfully considering your weaknesses, and look for habits and patterns that are holding you back. The adversary will not want you to make this list because as you pinpoint a weak spot, you will want to change. This list of weaknesses will be easier to compile if you have already made the list of your gifts, talents, and strengths. Following are a few suggestions that will help:

- Write in detail the short and long term cost of having each weakness (spiritual, emotional, physical)
- State who is responsible for your weaknesses
- Keep a journal to record your feelings regarding your weaknesses
- Begin working on the weakness that is holding you back the most
- Ask how overcoming this weakness will help you achieve your life mission.

Our weaknesses, like President Hinckley's impatience, are most likely associated with our life missions and can be turned into strengths with the Lord's help.

---

Notes

1. Neal A. Maxwell, *We Talk of Christ, We Rejoice in Christ*, 130.
2. Brigham Young, *Journal of Discourses*, 13:243, 252.
3. Edward L. and Andrew E. Kimball Jr., *Spencer W. Kimball: Twelfth President of The Church of Jesus Christ of Latter-day Saints*, 115.
4. Lynn G. Robbins, "Tithing—A Commandment Even for the Destitute," *Ensign*, April 2005, 36.
5. Sheri L. Dew, *Go Forward With Faith: The Biography of Gordon B. Hinckley*, 186.
6. Ibid., 164.
7. Ibid.
8. Clyde J. Williams, ed., *Teachings of Lorenzo Snow: Fifth President of The Church of Jesus Christ of Latter-day Saints*, 35.
9. Vincent Van Gogh, www.quotationspage.com.

# CHAPTER 6

―∞∞∞―

# DISCOVER WHY YOU ARE
# THE WAY YOU ARE

*We want every Latter-day Saint to come to the sacrament table because it is the place for self-investigation, for self-inspection, where we may learn to rectify our course and to make right our own lives, bringing ourselves into harmony with the teachings of the Church and with our brethren and sisters.*
—Bryant S. Hinckley

A BYU sociology professor, Dr. Reed Bradford, gave me an assignment that changed my life. It was one that he also had received while a PhD student at Harvard University, and it had changed his life, too: *"Write a ten-page paper describing why you are the way you are."*

Dr. Bradford gave our class almost no direction on how the paper was to be written. He said only that he wanted us to examine our past to see if there were things that were blocking our current progression. He mentioned a personal quality that he had pinpointed while writing his paper many years before; he realized that he was a yeller. Bothered by this weakness and worried that it could damage his young family, Dr. Bradford puzzled over why he yelled. He knew he raised his voice when he was frustrated, but that was a trigger, not the root reason behind this flaw. He decided he would talk to his father, who was also a yeller. His father didn't know why he yelled either, but mentioned that Grandpa was a yeller too. Finally, Dr. Bradford made the connection; yelling was a tradition in the Bradford home and had been passed through at least three generations.

When he fully realized what he was doing, he recognized the negative impact it was having on his family. He made a commitment after writing that paper that his yelling would stop—and it did.

Because Reed Bradford realized this weak spot in his character and its possible origins, he was able to confront the problem and eliminate it from his life. If he had continued to vent his frustration with shouting, I doubt he would have achieved his potential as a master teacher and mentor to people like me. Dr. Bradford received the Karl G. Maeser Distinguished Teaching Award and was included in the list of *Top 10 BYU Professors of the 20th Century.* Patiently influencing young people was his life mission.

With pen in hand, I sat down to begin my essay for Dr. Bradford. What did he mean by *"Why am I the way I am?"* My first answer was, "I was born that way." Then I began looking deeper into my past. Why, for example, did I lean toward a certain political philosophy? Was it because my father had indoctrinated me by discussing his political views at home? The more I thought about it, the more I could see that I had taken on many of my father's strengths and also several of his faults. I despaired that I was merely a clone of my parents. However, with the Lord's help, I realized that I had my own unique gifts, talents, and, unfortunately, weaknesses.

During the process of writing, the Lord helped me identify some things that were holding me back. Specifically, I realized that I was plagued by a destructive habit of worrying over even the smallest things. I reviewed scenes from my life to get to the root of the "worrying curse." First, I began with things I dreaded.

I hated Halloween and thought back to when this loathing began. My mother had been our ward Relief Society president for many of my growing up years. She sometimes took me along when she responded to the needs of the ward members. I will never forget accompanying her the night of October 31 when I was eleven years old. She was called to the home of some ward members to stay with their younger children while the parents dealt with a terrible family tragedy. Their son Robert, the senior class president that year, had been admiring a friend's new pistol. The friend was showing him how he could quick draw, but as he did, he accidentally shot Robert in the chest. He died instantly. In our hometown, we didn't leave the bodies of the dead in funeral homes so people could pay their respects there. Instead, the casket was brought to the family home for visitation. I was there when the friend who had shot Robert knelt beside the casket and begged Robert to get up. Each Halloween that heartbreaking scene and the cries of, "Please get up," ring in my head. Many years later I talked to someone who grew up with me in that ward, and she mentioned how she also disliked Halloween. Before I asked her why, I knew what her answer would be. She said Halloween reminded her of the night Robert died.

Tragedies such as the assassination of American president John F. Kennedy, the explosion of the space shuttle *Challenger*, and the terrorist attacks against America on September 11, 2001, are forever embedded in our memories. When traumatic events take place even closer to home, they can help explain why we are the way we are.

One day about a year after Robert died, I was crossing the highway in front of our home to catch the school bus. I looked to my right and saw that my eight-year-old neighbor Spencer was also crossing. I was aware of the bus approaching in the distance, but it was far enough away not to be a danger to either of us. I had reached the other side of the street when I heard brakes squealing. Spencer had turned back in the street to urge his siblings to hurry, and a car hit him. The bus arrived and pulled to a stop. Adults ran into the street. We school children were hustled onto the bus and told to continue on to school. As the bus pulled away, I saw my father and Spencer's father giving him a blessing, but I knew it was too late; he died at the scene.

My brother and sister were both in high school at that time. They were popular, had a car, and frequently were out late on weekend nights. I could never go to bed until they were both home. Sometimes I would go outside and pace back and forth praying for their safety as my parents slept peacefully. Often I knelt down by the road and begged the Lord to bring them home safely, especially if they were not home when I thought they should be. I imagined them dead a hundred times, with all of the wrenching emotions that went with that loss.

Years later, those obsessive behaviors resurfaced when my wife wasn't home at the hour I expected her, or when the time neared for our teenagers to return from dates. I was able to put this worrying behind me only after our children married and I did not know if they were out late or safely home in their beds.

There was a positive side to my worrying. I *always* came home at a decent hour and *always* told my parents where I would be. If an occasion arose where I would be late, I called to let them know. These experiences made me sensitive to my parents' feelings.

As I wrote my ten-page paper for Dr. Bradford's class, I began to realize the reasons behind my strong feelings. The environment in which I was raised, along with the events that made up my past, had a huge influence on how I act and react today. Once you come to an understanding of these reactions to past events, you can begin to work through and overcome those things that hold you back.

During one of our family reunions, our children and their spouses got into a lively discussion of the behaviors and attitudes that could be slowing their eternal progression, even things from their pasts. I shared with them some of the experiences that had changed my life, and I asked them to do the same. Our daughter Natalie told us about a time when she was in fourth grade. Two other Latter-day Saint friends, Melissa and Damon, had transferred out of the program for gifted and talented students and into Natalie's regular class that year. They were smart, and Natalie tried hard to keep up with them, but they always seemed to stay a step ahead of her, and the teacher lavished praise on them. Natalie said, "They beat me at everything!"

One day they were given a creative homework assignment by a student teacher. A picture of a hobo was distributed to students with the instruction to describe what they saw in such detail that someone could envision the hobo without seeing the picture. The next day the teacher used Natalie's paper as the example of what *not* to do. In front of everyone and in painful detail, the teacher told the class why it was not a good paper. Natalie ran out of the room and hid in a restroom stall for almost an hour while the student teacher frantically searched for her. Natalie said, "From that point on, I questioned everything I did in school. It became harder and harder to turn in assignments because I knew they wouldn't be quite good enough." She turned to art since it was one of her gifts in which she had confidence.

Neither my wife nor I had any idea why Natalie didn't like school or why she never wanted to write papers. All she wanted to do in school was draw. She is now married with two little children and is still a capable artist. But she is also a talented teacher and speaker to youth.

It is part of her life mission, discovered in spite of—or perhaps because of—an early setback that was strikingly similar to my own.

During that same family reunion, our youngest daughter Nichelle shared an experience she had on the first day of sixth grade. Our family had moved from Orem, Utah, to Austin, Texas. Nichelle had left some close friends behind. Sitting with her in the front seat of the car on the first morning of school, I reassured her that everything would be fine, and reminded her that she had already met a few girls her age at our new ward. I asked her what she was afraid of. "Going to lunch," came her reply. What she feared most was sitting in the lunchroom alone. I assured her that someone would want to sit by her, but I was wrong.

She told us at the family reunion what happened that day when she was just eleven years old. She walked to the lunchroom, but no one asked her to sit with her, so she sat by herself. Just as she began to eat her lunch, she looked up and saw a girl from the ward walking toward her with a friend. Her heart leapt, thinking she was about to be included. But, as the Latter-day Saint girl reached Nichelle's table, she sneered and said, "You don't have any friends, do you?" and continued walking to another table. I understand my daughter much better now and why, during the remainder of her school years, she preferred to stay home rather than seek friends who might reject her.

Why do these things happen? I don't have all the answers, but I know they can be related to our life missions. Nichelle is now married to her best friend and has two little girls. She loves teaching Primary children, always makes them feel welcome, and receives their love in return. Her experiences in life taught her to be that way.

When Nephi was discouraged about being angry with his brothers, he asked himself a series of questions: "And why should I yield to sin, because of my flesh? Yea, why should I give way to temptations, that the evil one have place in my heart to destroy my peace and afflict my soul? *Why am I angry* because of mine enemy?" (2 Nephi 4:27, emphasis added).

Nephi approached his anger using the same formula that Reed Bradford used to explore his yelling problem. He owned up to the problem and then was able to make commitments to himself and to the Lord to change.

### Nephi's Commitments to Self (vs. 28–30):

- "Awake, my soul!"
- "No longer droop in sin"
- "Give place no more for the enemy of my soul"
- "Do not anger again because of mine enemies"
- "Do not slacken my strength because of mine afflictions"
- "Rejoice, O my heart"
- "Cry unto the Lord"

### Nephi's Commitments to the Lord (vs. 30–35):

- "I will praise thee forever"
- "My soul will rejoice in thee, my God, and the rock of my salvation"
- "I will trust in thee forever"
- "I will not put my trust in the arm of flesh"
- "I will lift up my voice unto thee"
- "I will cry unto thee, my God"
- "My voice shall forever ascend up unto thee"

Nephi appears to have kept these commitments. Because he changed and overcame his anger problem, he became one of the great role models in history.

Sometimes life events spark intense desires within us that may well be part of the mission we were sent here to perform. These events may not require repentance, but may stimulate changes in our lives that connect us more closely to our life missions.

A remarkable woman from Norcross, Georgia, Becky Douglas, told me about her daughter Amber who had been a champion of the underdog, frequently bringing home people who needed help. Amber died when she was twenty-four years old. When Becky was going through her daughter's personal effects, she came across Amber's journal. From Amber's journal, Becky learned that Amber had donated money to a leper colony in India. Because Amber felt such a strong connection with these outcasts, Becky set up a fund in her daughter's memory to benefit the leper colony.

In 2001, Becky traveled to India to meet with the leaders of a leper organization. They immediately put her on their board of directors, and Becky passionately worked to make life better for them. Later she started her own charitable organization called "Rising Star Outreach." Through this nonprofit organization, lending groups distribute micro loans to those in the leper colonies. When the first small loan is repaid, the borrower can receive a bigger loan. For example, a man was given a $4 loan and bought a pot to make tea to sell to area farmers. When he paid back his loan, he was given an $8 loan and purchased a bike for delivering his tea. Today, he has four bikes with employees who sell his tea to farmers. This system has funded vegetable gardens, orchards, dairies, catfish ponds, art schools, and beauty shops.

Rising Star has also opened schools to educate children in leper colonies. Who would have dreamed that Amber Douglas's tragic death and journal account would have the influence it did? Who would have thought that a Georgia mother of nine would play such a vital role in the country of India?

During my conversation with Becky, I asked if she thought that Rising Star was her life mission. She said, "First, I'm a wife and a mother." She paused and then continued: "Yes, I think this is part of my life mission."[1] Nothing could replace the importance of the mission in her home, but Becky showed that with the Lord's help, capacities increase and talents can be used to bless those in an ever-widening circle of influence.

## Why Am I the Person I Am?

To understand who you can become, you must understand why you think and do the things you do. Spend a week thinking about all the reasons why you are the way you are. Think of your positive characteristics and the life events that may have helped you acquire them. Then think of weaknesses that hold you back and how they may have become part of your personality. Write down those reasons so you will better understand yourself. Several benefits will surface from this exercise. It not only will help you understand yourself, but it also can help others understand you. My wife and children became very sensitive to my worrying about them. They learned to call and let me know if they were going to be late.

Realizing that people are usually the way they are for a reason can help you be more understanding and less judgmental. I used to wonder why one of my friends would get so angry on the basketball court. Every time he was fouled, his face turned red and he doubled up his fists as if he wanted to fight. I finally understood when I learned that he had an abusive father who beat him regularly.

**For this exercise, ponder and consider the following ideas:**

- Can you identify the origin of your weakness?
- Were you born with this weakness?
- Was it passed down to you in your family environment?
- Was there an event or experience in your life that contributed to the way you react?

If you are to discover and achieve your life mission, you need to find out why you feel the way you do and why you do the things you do. Then you can make necessary changes or build on the firm personal foundation you create.

---

Note

1. Rising Star Outreach, http://www.risingstaroutreach.org.

# CHAPTER 7

# WRITE A PERSONAL
# MISSION STATEMENT

*If you don't know where you're going,
you might end up someplace else.*

—Yogi Berra

The mission statement of The Church of Jesus Christ of Latter-day Saints is brief, concise, and powerful: *"The three-fold mission of the Church is to proclaim the gospel, perfect the saints, and redeem the dead."* It is not vague nor is it embroidered. Our sacrament meetings, youth conferences, home teaching, temple worship, service projects, scouting, Sunday School, firesides, scripture study, and Family Home Evening all fit within this mission statement. Every Church meeting, every program, and every building derive their meaning and purpose from those few words.

Successful organizations and businesses also write mission statements—brief statements that sum up the fundamental purpose of a business, organization, or religious group. The statement clarifies why the organization exists and it keeps each member aware of that focus or objective. The following examples of mission statements tersely describe the purposes of these organizations:

> **Boy Scouts of America:** "To prepare young people to make ethical and moral choices over their lifetimes by instilling in them the values of the Scout Oath and Law."

**US Department of State:** "To create a more secure, democratic, and prosperous world for the benefit of the American people and the international community."

**Brigham Young University:** "To assist individuals in their quest for perfection and eternal life. That assistance should provide a period of intensive learning in a stimulating setting where a commitment to excellence is expected and the full realization of human potential is pursued."

**Ben and Jerry's Ice Cream:** "To make, distribute, and sell the finest quality all natural ice cream and euphoric concoctions with a continued commitment to incorporating wholesome, natural ingredients and promoting business practices that respect the earth and the environment."

**Occupational Safety & Health Administration (OSHA):** "To promote the safety and health of America's working men and women by setting and enforcing standards; providing training, outreach, and education; establishing partnerships; and encouraging continual process improvement in workplace safety and health."

**American Bible Society:** "To make the Bible available to every person in a language and format each can understand and afford, so all people may experience its life-changing message."

Yogi Berra once said: "If you don't know where you're going, you might wind up someplace else."[1] There is much truth to this adage. If an organization knows where it is going, it can more accurately plan the steps needed to reach its desired goals. Without that focus, how will the organization ever arrive where it desires to be? Just as organizations benefit from having mission statements, so can individuals. A personal mission statement is a concise written explanation of what you will achieve, what your focus will be, and what you will ultimately become. It is a tool to help you center your attention, energy, and actions on the things you consider most essential in your life.

We have all been sent to earth with a specific mission to perform. President Gordon B. Hinckley explained it this way: "Brethren and sisters, we're all part of one great family. Each has a duty; each has a mission to perform. And when we pass on, it will be reward enough if we can say to our beloved Master, 'I have fought a good fight, I have finished my course, I have kept the faith' " (2 Tim. 4:7).[2] Obtaining a body and being tested are the reason that every person is born into mortality. But the missions that President Hinckley speaks of are an additional purpose, unique to each of us. Your duty is to discover your individual mission and labor to accomplish it. In the process you will be preparing to meet God. "For behold, this life is the time for men to prepare to meet God; yea, behold the day of this life is the day for men to perform *their labors*" (Alma 34:32. emphasis added).

President David O. McKay gave Wendell B. Mendenhall a confidential assignment to select several likely spots for a temple to be built in New Zealand. In the April 1955 General Conference, Brother Mendenhall shared some of his experiences concerning that assignment:

"As President McKay told you, one of my assignments was to select several likely spots on which a temple could be built. Several spots which looked like they might be desirable were found, but as I was traveling in a car one afternoon I came upon another spot and without any question of a doubt I knew the reason why the temple should be there. I drove up over the top of a hill overlooking the area and my decision was confirmed."

Later President McKay came to New Zealand to review all the choices. "I had not said a word to him. No one else knew a thing," Brother Mendenhall said. "When President McKay looked around the area and saw this beautiful hill, he said, 'This is the place where the temple should be,' and this statement confirmed the thing which was in my heart. Then a week later President McKay came back to this beautiful spot and I bear witness to you, my brethren, that I saw the Prophet of this Church in the spirit of vision and when he walked away from that hill, he knew the House of the Lord was to be erected upon that particular spot." [3]

Wendell B. Mendenhall had a mission to perform, using his temporal skills and his spiritual gifts to help with the physical buildings of the Church in his capacity as chairman of the Church Building Committee. In 1962 he spoke at BYU:

"If I could, I would impress you students with these cardinal facts: (1) Each of you has a significant mission to perform. (2) Each of you has a purpose in life and God will help you to discover and understand your mission; He will help you find and understand your purpose. (3) He will bless you that you may fulfill your mission and achieve your purpose if you will but serve Him, keep His commandments, and diligently seek Him."[4]

It is not only prophets and apostles who are foreordained to have important assignments on earth. Elder Theodore M. Burton said, "According to the plan of salvation you were reserved or held back in the heavens as special spirit children to be born in a time and at a place where you could perform a special mission in life. This concept of being foreordained for a special mission is not new. It is referred to many times in the scriptures. Paul, in teaching the Ephesians, said: 'Blessed be the God and Father of our Lord Jesus Christ, who hath blessed us with all spiritual blessings in heavenly places in Christ: According as he hath chosen us in him before the foundation of the world, that we should be holy and without blame before him in love' " (Eph. 1:3–4).[5]

When formulated under the guidance of the Spirit, a personal mission statement helps give meaning to your life. By having one, you will be better able to judge if you have accomplished what you were sent here to do. It becomes easier to make decisions when you have a benchmark to measure whether a choice supports your life mission. When trials and adversity come into your life, which they will, having a purpose to focus on aids in putting things in proper perspective and helps get you through the tough times. Keeping a mission statement in front of you at all times also helps eliminate time-wasting activities and helps you focus on how best to use your time. It provides the push you need to be your best self since you know when you are not living up to your purpose. When you are true to your mission, you attract others around you who provide support to help you reach your destination. Memorizing your mission statement firmly stamps your purpose in your mind, to be recalled as you plan each day.

# Rules for a Good Mission Statement

The best mission statements are short and to the point. Most are no more than one or two sentences long. Some businesses state their mission in their name. Consider the restaurant chain Baja Fresh

Mexican Grill. The first word, *Baja,* tells you the type of food served; it is influenced by California Spanish cuisine and not Tex-Mex. The second word is *fresh.* A sign in all of their locations states that no can openers are ever used there. The third word says they serve *Mexican* food just so you are not confused about what you'll find when you walk in. The last word is *grill* and explains how they cook their food.

With much thought and prayer, you should be able to choose just a few words to accurately describe your life mission. Stephen R. Covey says, "Live life in crescendo."[6] That could easily be his mission statement. You should be able to put your purpose in life into a single sentence, commit it to memory, and have it constantly before you.

Consider the personal mission statements of these individuals:

**Jesus Christ:** "For behold, this is my work and my glory—to bring to pass the immortality and eternal life of man." (Moses 1:39)

**Nephi:** "For the fulness of mine intent is that I may persuade men to come unto the God of Abraham, and the God of Isaac, and the God of Jacob, and be saved." (1 Nephi 6:4)

**Joseph Smith:** "I made this my rule: When the Lord commands, do it." (*History of the Church,* 2:170)

We know why these men were sent to earth. But what are you expected to do with this mortal life? Do your daily life and decisions match your mission? A mission statement will help guide you. However, trying to develop one that encompasses all that you were sent to do can take effort. You are trying to discover your innermost desires, your gifts and talents, your weaknesses and your great interests. In some cases, you must turn up the soil on things about yourself that you have not previously acknowledged. Before writing something as important as a mission statement, ask yourself several questions:

- What brings me joy and happiness?
- What is my greatest desire?
- How do I like to spend my free time?
- What positive things have people said about me?
- What do I enjoy talking about with friends?

- If I had only one year to live, what would I want to do?
- If money were no object, what would I be doing with my life?

Write anything that comes to mind. At first your written mission statement might not seem to fit or be something you feel passionate about. Don't be discouraged; just keep writing. If you will pay the price in effort, one of your statements eventually will feel right. The answer will come as almost a whisper from another source. It will be a still yet distinct message that you are on the right path.

At BYU I was given an assignment in a sociology class that at first seemed macabre. Although the title of this assignment didn't say as much, I see now that our professor was trying to get us to discover our mission statements. Our assignment was to *write your own obituary*. I struggled with that assignment, unsure even of what an obituary should include beyond the circumstances of my death and a brief biography. So I turned to fiction, wavering between shameless flattery and brutal self-assessment. One imagined obituary went something like this: "Randal Wright died today of natural causes. He was the sorriest, no good, low down, lying, conniving, cheating, two bit scoundrel who ever lived on the earth. He had no wife or kids because he was too stingy to have them." In reality, if you don't give the end of your life much thought, the natural man may lead you aimlessly to this worst-case scenario.

How did I want to be remembered? The obituary assignment got me thinking about how I wanted my life story to read, and how far I was from that imagined life. I thought of others I admired and the qualities they had that I wanted in my own life. I thought about the roles that I then had and the ones I would have in the future: husband, father, friend, Church member, employee, citizen, and more. The assignment helped me realize that I didn't have my life mission fixed in my mind. I had a few bits and pieces, but the details were missing.

I challenge you to write your own obituary. Imagine yourself like the prophets of old, who, as they faced death, gathered their descendants and counseled them about the important things in life. What would your parting words be to your children? Imagine that one of your descendants asked you what one thing you were most proud of in life. Another wants to know, "What are you leaving behind?"

Upon completing this task, you will likely have all the information you need to write a draft copy of your mission statement. By now you should know what brings you joy and the kind of person you know you can be. The following steps can guide you in the development of your own mission statement.

- Carry a draft copy with you for a time while deciding if it covers all aspects of your life

- Add anything that makes it more complete while keeping it concise and focused

- Finally, write your final mission statement and commit it to memory

# Examples of Personal Mission Statements

- "I will help individuals realize that they have a specific mission to perform in life."

- "I will use my gifts and talents to help eliminate world hunger."

- "I will study successful families and apply the lessons in my own home and share the knowledge gained with all in my sphere of influence."

- "I will treat everyone as if they are the most important person in the world."

- "I will use my gift of writing to build the kingdom of God on earth."

- "I will never knowingly injure the feelings of another by careless or disrespectful words or actions."

- "I will help preschool children to see their infinite worth through the eyes of God."

- "I will be a voice for the unborn who cannot speak for themselves."

- "I will mourn with those that mourn and comfort those that stand in need of comfort, seeking opportunities to heal and redirect lost souls."

- "I will be known as a person of honor and integrity so others will be interested in the gospel of Jesus Christ because of my example."

- "With my Father in Heaven's help, I will stand as a witness of him at all times and in all things and in all places."

- "I will use my resources and intellect to find cures for diseases."

Use your mission statement as the standard by which you live your life. You will know when it is the right fit for you because it will inspire, motivate and excite you.

If The Church of Jesus Christ of Latter-day Saints, as an organization, has a written mission statement, then you should have one, too. Putting yours in writing can be one of the most important things you do in life.

---

Notes

1. Yogi Berra, quotationspage.com.
2. Gordon B. Hinckley, "Our Testimony to the World," *Ensign*, May 1997, 83.
3. Wendell B. Mendenhall, in Conference Report, April 1955, 4.
4. Wendell B. Mendenhall, "That Faith Might Also Increase in the Earth," *BYU Speeches of the Year*, December 5, 1962, 8.
5. Theodore M. Burton, "Salvation for the Dead—A Missionary Activity," *Ensign*, May 1975, 69.
6. Stephen R. Covey, leadernetwork.org.

# CHAPTER 8

⚯

# CREATE A VISION

*A target, to be hit, must be seen.*

Several years ago, an elderly wood carver in Spring, Texas, taught me something about envisioning my possibilities. I was with a group of seminary and institute teachers and their spouses at a convention, and we took a stroll through the streets of Old Spring, a collection of small, unique shops. One window that caught my interest was filled with exotic carvings. Upon entering the store, I saw an old wood carver sitting just inside the door. He was carving a large block of wood. Our group crowded into the store and gathered around as he stopped to show us some of his pieces. One was an intricately carved Native American chief.

Gazing appreciatively at this work of art, one member of our group asked, "How in the world did you accomplish this?" The old man replied, "Well, I'll tell you. I just carved away everything that wasn't an Indian chief, and this is what was left!" He had seen in his mind exactly what the final product should look like and worked until it matched that vision. It occurred to me that he could have created anything out of wood as long as he began with a vision.

The old man was echoing the more famous words of Italian sculptor Michelangelo, who frequently described his work similarly: "In every block of marble I see a statue as plain as though it stood before me, shaped and perfect in attitude and action. I have only to hew away the rough walls that imprison the lovely apparition to reveal it to the other eyes as mine see it." And, "I saw the angel in the marble and carved until I set him free."

To be set free to become your best self, you must be able to envision the possibilities. Vision is defined as the act or power of anticipating that which will or may come to be. One woman gifted with such vision was Helen Keller. Because of a severe illness, she became blind and deaf at eighteen months of age. When Helen was about seven years old, Anne Sullivan, who was only twenty at the time, became her teacher and friend. They were inseparable until Anne's death in 1936. Helen graduated Cum Laude from Radcliffe College, becoming the first blind and deaf person ever to graduate from college. She authored twelve books and inspired millions of people. A reporter once asked Helen how it felt to not see her dreams being fulfilled. She replied, "The only thing worse than being blind is having eyes to see, but having no vision."[1]

Do we have eyes to see where we are going in life? Helen Keller helped people throughout the world create the vision of who they could become. She felt as President Spencer W. Kimball did when he said, "The problems of the world cannot possibly be solved by skeptics or cynics whose horizons are limited by the obvious realities. We need men who can dream of things that never were and ask, 'Why not?' "[2]

And then there are those who simply say, "Not me."

Elder Merlin R. Lybbert of the Seventy told the following story: "An enterprising turkey gathered the flock together and, following instructions and demonstrations, taught them how to fly. All afternoon they enjoyed soaring and flying and the thrill of seeing new vistas. After the meeting, all of the turkeys walked home."[3] You may have experienced moments when visionaries have taught you how to fly. However, when your time has come to soar, you have doubted your abilities and remained earthbound. "Where there is no vision, the people perish" (Proverbs 29:18).

Sam Walton, the founder of Wal-Mart once said, "Capital isn't scarce; vision is."[4]

There is no scarcity of vision in a little country in the Middle East called Dubai. It has a population of 857,233 and is ruled by His Highness Shaikh Mohammad Bin Rashid Al Maktoum. In March 2000, the shaikh told London's *Sunday Telegraph* newspaper, "I have a vision. I look to the future, 20, 30 years."[5] His vision for the country seems impossible in scope and execution, given that Dubai does not have the vast oil resources of its rich neighbors. Yet, if the ambitious shaikh can realize his vision, sandy and barren Dubai will have: A cluster of man-made islands dredged from the sea and designed to resemble the continents of the world, another cluster of islands shaped to look from the air like a palm tree, the largest shopping mall in the world, the world's tallest sky scraper (2,640 feet), an amusement park twice the size of Disney World, an indoor ski mountain, the first underwater luxury hotel, the largest fully-automated rail system in the world, and the world's largest airport.

You don't have to be a shaikh or build a city in the desert to be a visionary. The results of vision are everywhere. Some recognize that a target, to be hit, must be seen. Members of the Church are blessed with examples of leaders with tremendous vision. What they clearly demonstrate is that when we involve the Lord in our lives and stay close to him, he will inspire us with the exact details of what our future should hold.

Consider the vision and life missions of Joseph Smith and Brigham Young. Wilford Woodruff described the vision of Joseph Smith. The year was 1833, just three years after the Church was organized. One Sunday night the prophet gathered priesthood holders into a fourteen-foot-square log schoolhouse to be taught and edified. Several of those gathered bore testimony of the work in which they were engaged. Then the prophet spoke. "Brethren I have been very much edified and instructed in your testimonies here tonight, but I want to say to you before the Lord, that you know no more concerning the destinies of this Church and kingdom than a babe upon its mother's lap. You don't comprehend it. . . . It is only a little handful of Priesthood you see here tonight, but this Church will fill North and South America—it will fill the world. . . . It will fill the Rocky Mountains. There will be tens of thousands of Latter-day Saints who will be gathered in the Rocky Mountains. . . . This people will go into the Rocky Mountains; they will there build temples to the Most High."[6] It is apparent from this statement and the setting that by 1833 Joseph knew what his mission included and could see the vision of what the Church would become.

Nine years later, the Prophet Joseph issued an even more famous statement concerning the destiny of the Church and the vision he had of its future: "Our missionaries are going forth to different nations. . . .

The standard of truth has been erected; no unhallowed hand can stop the work from progressing, persecutions may rage, mobs may combine, armies may assemble, calumny may defame, but the truth of God will go forth boldly, nobly, and independent, till it has penetrated every continent, visited every clime, swept every country, and sounded in every ear, till the purposes of God shall be accomplished and the great Jehovah shall say the work is done."[7]

Brigham Young also was a visionary. We can see the results of his vision for the Salt Lake Valley. Because of harsh conditions encountered for a time, many of the pioneers wanted to leave the valley to seek their fortunes in California. President Hinckley described the scene and the future reflected in Brigham's eyes:

> In 1849, two years after our people first arrived here and following the discovery of gold in California, many were discouraged. They had struggled to wrest a living from the arid soil. Crickets had devoured their crops. The winters were cold. Many thought they would go to California and get rich. President Young stood before them and encouraged them to remain, promising that "God will temper the climate, and we shall build a city and a temple to the Most High God in this place. We will extend our settlements to the east and west, to the north and to the south, and we will build towns and cities by the hundreds, and thousands of the Saints will gather in from the nations of the earth. This will become the great highway of the nations. Kings and emperors and the noble and wise of the earth will visit us here.[8]

On a visit to Salt Lake City, I scanned the landscape before me with its tall buildings, wide streets and masses of people. I thought about Brigham Young standing in sagebrush making that statement. I'm sure there were many who thought there was no possible way his vision could materialize. Yet everything he said came true in dramatic fashion. Note in the following examples how the vision was fulfilled:

- **"God will temper the climate."** God tempered not only the climate, but the soil also, and the Saints found that it would produce not just sagebrush, but also fruits and vegetables in abundance. Over the years I have planted many gardens in many places. The best ones by far have been in Utah.

- **"We shall build a city."** Although a few Saints left for California and its mild climate and gold, the vast majority stayed in the Salt Lake Valley and built a beautiful city. It has now become a world-class city in many ways. As of 2008, the Salt Lake City metropolitan area had an estimated population of 1,018,826. More than four million people ski its resorts every year. Seven of the largest industrial banks in the United States are in Utah, including the three largest.

- **"And a temple to the Most High God."** Brigham Young announced the temple on July 26, 1847. He planted his cane on the ground and said, "Here we will build the temple of our God."[9] He also proclaimed, "We are building this temple to stand through the millennium."[10] Elder John A. Widtsoe said of Brigham Young, "At the laying of the cornerstones of the Salt Lake Temple, he told the people that in vision he had seen the completed temple. It would have six towers he said, three at each end."[11] Brigham Young never got to see the finished temple and its towers that he saw in vision, nor did he live to see another of his visions come to fruition: "This is not the only temple we shall build; there will be hundreds of them built and dedicated to the Lord."[12]

- **"We will extend our settlements to the east and west, to the north and to the south, and we will build towns and cities by the hundreds, and thousands of the saints will gather in from the nations of the earth."** We have evidence that Brigham Young "oversaw the gathering of nearly one hundred thousand Latter-day Saints to the valleys of the Rocky Mountains and colonized some four hundred cities and towns. He built temples and tabernacles, organized stakes and wards throughout the western United States, and sent missionaries to nearly every corner of the United earth." [13]

- **"Kings and emperors and the noble and wise of the earth will visit us here."** Salt Lake City is a frequent stop for kings, emperors, presidents, scientists, and politicians. During the 2002 Olympic Games, seventy-seven nations and 2,399 athletes participated with their kings and emperors in attendance.

There is much you can learn from people with vision. They are able to see in their minds the work they have to do. They also see details that must be considered, including the resources at their disposal, in order to make the vision a reality. When others are enlisted to make the vision happen, visionary leaders are able to communicate the vision to them and inspire them to help accomplish it.

Elder Vaughn J. Featherstone gave insights into visualizing future goals and aspirations. He said, "Those who have vision have many things in common:

- They see the total work before them.

- They visualize what must happen in order to get the results they desire.

- They consider all of their resources, potentials, and capabilities collectively.

- They see in their mind what marvelous and magnificent things could happen when the total work force is mobilized unitedly

- They then go to work to accomplish their goal.

- They have the ability to communicate their vision to those around them in a convincing way so that others are enlisted also.

- They see what they are doing as a cause, not a project."[14]

You are limited not by your abilities but by your vision. French writer Antoine de Saint Exupéry said, "A rock pile ceases to be a rock pile the moment a single man contemplates it, bearing within him the image of a cathedral."[15] Spend time pondering what your vision is to accomplish those things you have been sent to earth to do. The Lord has placed a pile of rocks in front of you. He expects you to see in your mind's eye the cathedral you are to build and he expects you to pick up your tools and work toward its completion.

---

Notes

1. Helen Keller, www.goodreads.com.
2. Spencer W. and Edward L. Kimball, *The Teachings of Spencer W. Kimball*, 487.
3. Merlin R. Lybbert, "A Latter-day Samaritan," *Ensign*, May 1990, 81.
4. Sam Walton, quotationsbook.com.
5. Shaikh Mohammad Bin Rashid Al, archive.gulfnews.com.
6. Wilford Woodruff, in Conference Report, April 1898, 57.
7. Joseph Smith, *History of the Church*, 4:540.
8. Gordon B. Hinckley, "The Church Goes Forward," *Ensign*, May 2002, 4.
9. James H. Anderson, "The Salt Lake Temple," *Contributor*, April 6, 1893, 243.
10. LeGrand Richards, "Laying a Foundation for the Millennium," *Ensign*, December 1971, 81.
11. John A. Widtsoe, *Evidences and Reconciliations: Aids to Faith in a Modern Day*, 49.
12. Brigham Young, *Discourses of Brigham Young*, 395.
13. Brigham Young, *Teachings of Presidents of the Church: Brigham Young*, 111.
14. Vaughn J. Featherstone, *The Incomparable Christ: Our Master and Model*, 113.
15. Antone de Saint Exupéry, deSaintExupéry,poetry2share.proboards79.com.

# CHAPTER 9

# SET AND ACHIEVE WORTHWHILE GOALS

*Not failure, but low aim is often our greatest sin.*

—Elder LeGrand Richards

One day I stopped by the neighborhood mailbox to pick up my mail. A woman joined me at the box with her little boy. He was pleading with her to let him open their box, so she handed him the key. When he peeked in the box he let out a squeal of delight and I was immediately curious about what was in there. He was too young to read so I knew he couldn't be gushing over the winning entry for the Publishers Clearing House Sweepstakes. "We got them, we got them!" he shouted as he jumped up and down. As I looked down at his little pile of mail, I saw the source of his giddy excitement. He was clutching two movies from an online movie rental service. The little boy looked up at his mother and exclaimed, "This is the best day of my life!" I offered some advice to his mother, "You need to get this boy a more exciting life." She laughed and agreed with my assessment.

Like the little boy with the movies, many adults also need to "get a life." While visiting friends, I watched a TV program about the Guinness Book of World Records. One man featured on the program put tarantulas in his mouth and another ran a drill up his nose. But the portion of the program that stuck most in my memory was the man who set the record for keeping the most basketballs spinning at once. After the admittedly impressive feat, the champion spinner was interviewed by the host and asked how he felt. He replied, "This is the greatest day of my life." Here was a married man with children, and, for him, spinning basketballs constituted the greatest day of his life. I wondered how his wife and children felt.

When the "highlights" reel is played for your life, what will the best days be? For too many adults, the most exciting things in life are the new movie or video game, or the adrenalin rush of a shopping spree. I have talked to people who still manage to bring into our conversations the high school football game that they almost won forty years previously. While I don't discount the value of simple pleasures and accomplishments, we often rely on past achievements or brushes with greatness to make present life meaningful. Napoleon Dynamite's self absorbed Uncle Rico wishes he could go back in time for his chance at fame and fortune. If the coach only would have put him in, he would have won the state championship and gone on to play for the National Football League. Instead of looking to achieve something meaningful in the future, he dwells on past "could have beens." Although it's fun to reminisce, it can be unhealthy to live in the past. Our focus should be on setting goals that head us in the proper direction for our future.

The word *goal* is a modern word meaning an end or objective, and although the word is not found in the scriptures, many passages allude to goal setting. "Be ye therefore perfect" (Matthew 5:48) and "seek ye first the kingdom of God" (Matthew 6:33) are examples of what our Heavenly Father regards as essential goals. Worthy goals give purpose and meaning to life. The lack of goals creates turmoil and indecision, often necessitating a return to the past to bring present satisfaction.

## THE VALUE OF SETTING GOALS

As critical as goals are to accomplishing anything of worth, most people do not consciously make goals. For many, failure to achieve success can be traced directly to not having any goals or having only vague goals. Elder Neal A. Maxwell shared this thought. "An unwillingness to set standards or goals for ourselves, of course, can result in a Mormon malaise, going nowhere but very anxiously."[1]

Years ago my daily drive to work took me by the port in Beaumont,

Texas, where I saw ships from all over the world anchored. Imagine being a sailor on one of those ships as it pulled out into the Gulf of Mexico and asking the captain what his destination was. And then imagine him saying, "I have no idea! We are just going to see where the currents take us." That is not far removed from the way some people live. Elder LeGrand Richards said, "If we don't know where we came from, and we don't know why we are here, and we don't know where we are going, nor how to get there, we are just like a ship on the ocean without a rudder, or a sail, or anyone to guide it. We might keep afloat, but we would never come into port."[2] If you are to protect yourself in this day of spiritual and moral decay, and reach your divine destiny, you must know where you are going. People who set goals in life are more likely to succeed because they know where they are going.

In the spring of 1973, I was sitting in an organizational behavior class taught by Steven R. Covey. This was years before his best-selling book *Seven Habits of Highly Effective People* was published. I envied him in many ways. He had grown up in a home where education was stressed. He obtained an MBA from Harvard University. He was teaching college students from across the nation and having a tremendous influence in their lives. He was also a successful and respected business consultant and owned his own firm. He seemed to know what his mission was, and he was on the path to accomplishing it.

My background was quite different. My father was number eight of eleven children and was raised by an alcoholic father in a logging camp on the Texas/Louisiana border. He had a sixth grade education, although he was very bright and loved to learn. My mother grew up in rural Alabama, the oldest of four living children. When she was a thirteen-year-old eighth grader, her mother went to the hospital to give birth to another child. She had previously lost four children in childbirth, so there was the ever-present worry that it would happen again. Word came that my grandmother did lose her fifth baby that day, but this time was different, because she died too. The family grieved terribly, and my mother was forced to drop out of school to care for her three younger siblings while her father worked in the fields.

Although my parents were wonderful people, we did not grow up talking about Plato or Shakespeare around the dinner table.

As I sat in Stephen Covey's class, I dreamed of what I could become as this brilliant professor inspired me with visions of the future. He spoke of winning private victories before we could win public victories. One day he asked us what we would be doing in ten years. Other than my junior high fantasy of playing professional football or basketball, I had never seriously considered what my long-range future would hold. However, that semester I took an index card and wrote down what I hoped to be doing in 1983. I privately wished I could teach college-age students as he did, but that seemed impossible because of my background and grades. I wasn't even confident that I could get my bachelor's degree, much less the advanced degrees required to teach at the college level. So instead, I decided to aim for having my own business one day in Texas. I wrote that down along with several other modest goals. That little card got shoved into a stack with other semester notes. My conscious mind forgot about those dreams and goals, and I got back to the daily grind.

I did graduate with a degree in business and family science and moved back to Texas. During the move, those written goals were misplaced and assumed lost. The next ten years passed quickly. I was married with a family and lived in southeast Texas, where I had grown up. I taught early morning seminary and was part of our family business. One day my mother asked me if I wanted something I had left in a closet at her home. She handed me that index card from 1973. I can still remember the excitement at seeing my list of goals and realizing that I was doing every single thing I had written down ten years earlier. By writing down my goals, I had internalized them, even though I had lost the card and forgotten the words.

For weeks I was on a high, relishing the fact that I had accomplished everything I set out to do. Over time, however, a new feeling began to set in: "What's next?" It was exhilarating to have accomplished the things on my ten-year list, but I was only thirty-five years old and had no idea what to do with the next ten years.

## THINKING BIG

About that time I read a newspaper article about a world explorer named John Goddard, a Latter-day Saint living in California. When John was fifteen years old, he recorded 127 goals that he planned to accomplish in life. As I read his list of planned adventures, I was taken aback at what he had already accomplished. There was little on his list that I wanted to do, but it gave me the impetus to start my own list. Some of John's life adventures included:

- **Explore Rivers:** Nile, Amazon, Congo, Colorado, Yangtze, Niger, Orinoco, Rio Coco

- **Study Primitive Cultures:** The Congo, New Guinea, Brazil, Borneo, Sudan, Kenya

- **Climb Mountains:** Everest, McKinley, Kilimanjaro, Ararat, Cook, Matterhorn, Rainier, Fuji

- **Photograph:** Victoria Falls, Sutherland Falls, Yosemite Falls, Niagara Falls

- **Explore:** Coral Reefs of Florida, Great Barrier Reef, Red Sea, Fiji Islands, Bahamas

- **Visit:** North/South Pole, Great Wall of China, Panama and Suez Canals, Easter Island, Vatican

- **Swim in Lake:** Victoria, Superior, Tanganyika, Titicaca, Nicaragua

- **Other:** Visit every country, become an Eagle Scout, play flute and violin, mission, write a book

Reading Goddard's list did something to me. I realized that his goals were far more exotic than anything I had ever even dreamed of, and a light went on in my head. "Do you mean I can set goals that seem unattainable?" Although few of John's goals interested me, he taught me to dream big. What did I have to lose? Reading his goals, I became even more dissatisfied with my mundane life and where I was headed. I felt like I was not doing what I was sent to do.

Questions popped into my head. What was I going to do with the rest of my life? Have I already accomplished the mission I was sent to do? Memories flooded back to me of the night in 1973 when I sat in the waiting room at the Utah Valley hospital. I made a promise to the Lord then that I would study families and share that information with others to help families stay together. I became more and more dissatisfied with my life, but I had no idea where to turn.

For weeks I thought about almost nothing else. Who was I? Was there such a thing as a life mission, and, if so, did I have one? I reread my patriarchal blessing, pondered and prayed for weeks, and finally decided to write down new goals—not for ten years, but for the rest of my life. If John Goddard could come up with 127 life adventures, then I could come up with 100. I thought about my strengths, weaknesses and desires. I reviewed my earlier college assignment to assess the events in my past and their impact on who I was. Finally, I began to write down a plan built on 100 life goals. Several things on my list were just dreams or desires. I didn't think they would come to pass, but I wrote them down anyway. Here is a partial list:

- Become an institute director
- Climb Mount Timpanogos
- Visit Hawaii Temple
- Write multiple books on the family
- Teach at BYU Education Week
- See all my children marry in the temple
- Teach at Especially for Youth
- Buy a 1970 Oldsmobile 442
- Have an article printed in the *Ensign*
- Visit all 50 states
- Become expert in electronic media effects
- Attend session of general conference
- Obtain masters degree
- Visit the Sacred Grove
- Earn a PhD
- Travel to the Holy Land
- Teach at least one class at BYU
- Speak for "Know Your Religion"

Many years have passed and I have learned for myself the power of dreaming dreams and setting goals as I have checked off the things on my list one by one.

A year after putting my goals on paper, I was still involved in the family business and teaching early morning seminary—sixteen seniors at 5:55 AM. Our class set a very difficult goal for the year, one that seemed impossible to achieve. At seminary graduation that year, the stake president said, "We would like to congratulate the seniors in Randal Wright's class. Each of them has earned 100 percent attendance for the entire school year." The *Church News* picked up on the story and published an article on our class.[3] Also, the personnel manager for the Church Educational System flew from Salt Lake City to visit our class. After the school year ended, he offered me a job with CES, and that fall I became the institute director at Lamar University, in Beaumont, Texas, fulfilling the first of my 100 life goals, a little more than a year after I wrote it down. Since the university was right across the street from the institute, I applied to the family studies program and obtained a master's degree, with an emphasis on the influence of television on families.

In 1986, I spoke at the Especially for Youth session in San Diego, California, the first EFY ever held outside of Utah. The next year I was the session director for the first EFY held in Texas. In 1987, my father in-law gave my wife and me frequent flyer miles for a trip to Hawaii, and while there, we attended the temple. At the same time my writing was catching the attention of publishers. The *Ensign* published a short article by me.[4] Then Deseret Book published my first book on families.[5] Later, I was able to attend BYU to work on a doctorate in family studies. My dissertation was on the influence of the electronic media on teenagers.[6] I taught in the BYU religion department during those years. Since we lived in Utah, my boys and I climbed Mount Timpanogos. I have been amazed and humbled at how opportunities presented themselves to achieve the goals I set back in 1985.

## SPIRITUAL DIRECTION

Goal setting has fallen on hard times among some in our society who would rather take life as it comes. Even active Church members have been heard to say that they would rather let the Spirit freely guide them, as if setting goals could not be compatible with spiritual promptings. Goals are dismissed as the purview of materialists and overachievers. Serendipity is touted as a better way to go.

But multiple prophets have counseled us to set goals, promising great blessings for doing so. President Ezra Taft Benson, for example, gave this counsel. "Every accountable child of God needs to set goals, short- and long-range goals. A man who is pressing forward to accomplish worthy goals can soon put despondency under his feet, and once a goal is accomplished, others can be set up."[7]

Elder Richard G. Scott said, "Establish specific objectives, and move steadily toward them. A rudder won't control a drifting boat; it must be underway. Similarly, you need to be moving forward to gain control of your life."[8]

While teaching at BYU, I gave my students an optional assignment to write their 100 life goals. There is nothing magical about the number, but I have found that the challenge of reaching 100 will prompt you to seek the Lord's advice when you quickly run out of your own ideas. The Lord knows what he wants you to do, and what you are capable of achieving. Out of the hundreds of students who completed this assignment, only a few had goals in common with the others. There were literally thousands of different goals mentioned by the combined group. I'm convinced they had divine help coming up with their lists. Here is the list of fifty goals a young returned missionary set:

Marry in the temple
Climb Mount Timpanogos in Utah
Baptize and confirm all my children
Learn to play jazz piano
Road tour all 50 states with family
Play piano while my wife sings
Visit Sacred Grove/bear testimony to family
Write in my journal every day
Attend general conference
Stay under 190 pounds
Serve a full-time mission with my wife
Exercise at least three times a week
Complete a college degree
Never watch an R-rated movie
Pray on the Mount of Olives
Have one year's food supply
Go to Singapore on my honeymoon

Learn to speak/write fluently in Spanish
Every Christmas help someone anonymously
Memorize one scripture per week
Help all my boys become Eagle Scouts
Write a talk every fast Sunday
Start a business
Read patriarchal blessing once a week
Land an airplane
Never use profanity
Establish mission/college funds for children
Introduce self to new people at church
Go river rafting
Take vocal lessons
Have daily prayer
Teach at the college level
Go on a 50-mile hike with my sons
Have something published
Hold family home evening every week
Run for public office
Tell family members I love them every day
Fast every fast Sunday
Take my wife on a date every weekend
Make monthly temple trip
Always maintain 100% home teaching
Invent something
Teach children to read before kindergarten
Learn sign language
Never go to bed angry with family member
Never own a television
Buy and restore a '54 Chevy convertible
Read a good book monthly
Write special book for parents about memories
Live every day as if last

Joel Hawes, an eighteenth century Massachusetts clergyman and writer, once said, "Aim at the sun, and you may not reach it; but your arrow will fly far higher than if aimed at an object on a level with yourself."[9] A better statement might begin with "Aim at the Son." All too often we are content to live as our acquaintances do when we are admonished to live as Christ did. Elder LeGrand Richards said, "Not failure, but low aim is often our greatest sin."[10] Jesus Christ is the sure foundation on which we are to build our lives.

## CHALLENGE: 100 LIFE GOALS

I challenge you to pull out your patriarchal blessing and study it once more. Ask Heavenly Father what goals he wants and needs you to set. Look closely at the mission statement you formulated to make sure your goals are in harmony with your life mission. My professor Stephen R. Covey taught, "Be sure that, as you scramble up the ladder of success, it is leaning against the right building."[11]

Now, prayerfully start writing your 100 life goals. Remember that an unwritten goal is just a wish and will soon be forgotten. Keep your list in a place where you will see it often. You will be amazed at how your life will steer toward your goals and how opportunities will arise to accomplish them.

Notes

1. Neal A. Maxwell, *Deposition of a Disciple*, 71–72.
2. LeGrand Richards, "What the Gospel Teaches," *Ensign*, May 1982, 29.
3. "Most Important Class Applauded," *LDS Church News*, June 16, 1985.
4. Randal A. Wright, "Our Family's Reverence Lesson," *Ensign*, August 1986, 43–44.
5. Randal A. Wright, *Families in Danger: Protecting Your Family in an X-rated World*.
6. Randal A. Wright, "Family, Religious, Peer, and Media Influence on Adolescence Willingness to Have Premarital Sex" (PhD dissertation), Brigham Young University, 1995.
7. Ezra Taft Benson, "Do Not Despair," *Ensign*, October 1986, 5.
8. Richard G. Scott, "Finding the Way Back," *Ensign*, May 1990, 74.
9. *The International Dictionary of Thoughts*, 26.
10. LeGrand Richards, "We Have to Pay the Price," Brigham Young University devotional, October 24, 1967.
11. Stephen R. Covey, quotationcollection.com.

# CHAPTER 10

# Obtain the Education Needed to Succeed

*Chance always favors the prepared life.*
—President Howard W. Hunter

Gene was fourteen when I first met him. He lived with his mother and had not come from a family where church attendance was a priority. But he happened to be at church one Sunday, and after the regular meetings were over, the youth of the ward gathered for an orientation meeting for an upcoming youth conference. My wife and I were there as specialists for the conference, and Wendy spotted Gene slipping out the front door of the chapel before the orientation. "Where are you going Gene?" she asked. "You don't want to miss the youth conference meeting."

Gene informed her that he wasn't going. "You are too going!" Wendy replied. A huge smile came over Gene's face, even though he tried to act as if he wasn't interested. Wendy gently steered him into the room where the meeting was being held. Gene did attend the youth conference and, from my perspective, it looked as if he was having more fun than any person there. He made lifelong friends that weekend, and a spark of testimony was ignited. He later went on a mission and married in the temple.

After graduating from BYU with a bachelor's degree in history, Gene was accepted to a prestigious graduate school to pursue a master's degree in business administration (MBA). After his first semester in a two-year program, he came home for Christmas and it was apparent he was under a lot of stress. He described to me how hard his graduate program was, pointing out his lack of a business background and the failure of his undergraduate work to prepare him for advanced business courses. Most students in the program had degrees in related fields or years of experience in the work force and were far better prepared for the rigors of the program. I asked him what he thought he should do. He felt he should quit.

I pondered what to say to this young man who had come to me for advice. When I asked how his mother and friends felt about this decision, he replied, "They said if it's too hard, then I should quit." In Gene's mind, it would take a miracle for him to finish the degree. I asked him what he would do with his history degree if he were to drop out of the MBA program. He thought his best option was to obtain a teaching certificate. That was a great option if that was what the Lord wanted him to do. But why, when he had prayed, had he received an answer that he should attend business school? He admitted he really wanted an MBA to make enough money to sustain his family, but also to generously support the Church and the missionary program.

I posed a question: "Gene, would you stay in the program if someone offered you a million dollars to finish?"

"If I could get a million dollars to finish, then I would stick with it no matter how hard it was."

At that point I pulled out a chart from a national magazine showing the career earnings for different degrees and occupations. First, we looked up his bachelor's degree and the average career earnings for a high school teacher. Then we turned to the average salary one would earn with an MBA from the university he was attending. The difference between the two was just over a million dollars in lifetime earnings. Gene decided to stay in the program. A year and a half later, he was awarded his graduate degree and accepted a job with a respected national company. Today Gene is the senior vice president of human resources for a $1.7 billion-a-year company. He is building up the Lord's kingdom as he said he would, in many more ways than with money alone.

This outcome is similar to the one the Lord promises you. If you have righteous desires and work hard to do his will, you will reap eternal rewards. It will not be easy; sometimes you will want to give up. But faith really does precede the miracle. "Therefore, prepare ye the way of the Lord, for the time is at hand that all men shall reap a reward of their works, according to that which they have been—if they have been righteous they shall reap the salvation of their souls, according to the power and deliverance of Jesus Christ" (Alma 9:28).

In the previous chapter, I shared some of the goals that one of my BYU students set. Assume for a moment that everything he put on his list was inspired and related to the mission he was sent to earth to accomplish. What price would he have to pay in education alone? Let's look at just one of his goals and consider for a moment what would be needed in terms of education. The student said he wanted to start a business. Many people, at some point in life, have this desire. For most, it is a just a dream, and they never do anything about it. Others actually start the business but fail because they are not sufficiently educated.

For a business to succeed, you have to find a need or niche and know how to fill it. To do that, a detailed business plan to determine the chances of success is needed. It takes a certain amount of education and there is always risk involved. Something as simple as naming a business is a complicated art form. Following are just a few of the subjects in which an entrepreneur needs expertise:

- **Name:** legal requirements, registration, domain names

- **Finance and Accounting:** start up costs, estimation cost, break-even analysis, equity capital, finding capital, billing, purchasing, accounts receivable, balance sheet, income statement, cash flow analysis, sales and expense forecast, securing capital needed, budgeting and managing company growth

- **Marketing:** target market, product development, pricing and payment options, media relations, finding customers, customer service and customer relations, networking, advertising, special events

- **Employees:** interviewing, hiring, job descriptions, pay, benefits, insurance, background checks, firing

- **Leadership:** mentoring, networking, roundtables, sharing vision, delegating, training, positive environment, encouraging productivity

- **Government:** local, state and federal taxes, employer ID, employee withholding, matching Social Security payments, tax forms, government regulations, business permits

- **Insurance:** general liability, product liability, workers compensation, malpractice

- **Building:** location, traffic flow, accessibility, parking, lighting, building safety, location of competition

- **Other:** fraud protection, production, equipment, suppliers, lawsuits, market trends

If a portion of your life mission is to open a business, you need to be educated in business dealings first. If your mission is to become a teacher, then you need to learn how to teach. If it is to be a brain surgeon, you need to know everything possible about the brain. While asking the Lord what I should do with my life, I felt a strong desire and need to conduct research on the influence that electronic media has on people. It seemed that the media was negatively impacting individuals and families. I felt the need to do my part in helping and protecting families from its influence. I did some research while an undergraduate but didn't know that much, and I'm sure no one would have listened to me had I tried to share the results. In time, I began to have a strong desire to get a master's degree and then a PhD in family studies, with an emphasis in electronic media. This gave me the desire to write a few books and speak around the nation on this subject. That would never have happened had I not pursued the education to open the window of opportunity.

On September 29, 1978, President Spencer W. Kimball spoke to the regional representatives of the Church. Elder Dallin H. Oaks was in attendance at that meeting and said, "President Kimball spoke of our obligation to take the gospel to what he called 'the uttermost parts of the earth' (see Doctrine and Covenants 58:64). His message was electrifying. No one who was present will ever forget the witness they felt that this was a prophet giving the Lord's message to the leaders and members of his restored Church. . . . The prophet pleaded for us to move forward, saying, 'It is better for something to be *underway* than under *advisement*.' He referred to various nations where we had not yet taught the restored gospel."[1]

During that meeting President Kimball emphasized the importance of having the work in China go forward and encouraged more members to learn to speak Mandarin Chinese. I'm sure many thought that request a little ambitious since at that time the United States had no diplomatic relations with China and foreign visitors were not encouraged. One person who took the message seriously was internationally known heart surgeon Russell M. Nelson. He had paid a tremendous price to be educated. He not only had a medical degree but a PhD as well. And even though he was extremely busy, he felt a special prompting to learn Mandarin Chinese.

That prompting was related to his life mission to help take the gospel to the world. R. Lanier Britsch later wrote, "Elder Russell M. Nelson, before and since his call as an Apostle in April 1984, has taught heart surgery at the Shandong Medical College in Jinan, Shandong Province. For service rendered in 1980 and 1984, he was named honorary professor in September 1984. His service and dedication to doing his teaching well were exceptional. He studied Mandarin Chinese and became proficient enough to communicate effectively, 'particularly during surgery.' His ability to speak and understand Chinese has helped, because he has visited China on several occasions since that time."[2]

Today the Church has a good relationship with the Chinese government. BYU touring groups have performed on several occasions and many of our members teach at Chinese universities. The Church has come to China's aid during times of need. Part of the credit for the warm relations between the Church and China goes to a busy heart surgeon who felt a prompting to learn Mandarin Chinese.

Hank Aaron was one of the greatest baseball players in history. For years he held the all-time record for home runs. He was also a man of great character. When he was young, however, he did not understand the importance of education and wanted to quit school so he could concentrate more on baseball. President Thomas S. Monson relates this story about him, "One day Hank said to his dad, 'I'm going to quit school, Dad. I'm going to go to work so I can play baseball.' And Herbert Aaron said to his son, 'My boy, I quit school because I had to, but you're not going to quit school. Every morning of your young life I've put fifty cents on the table that you might buy your lunch that day. And I take twenty-five cents with me, that I might buy my lunch. Your education means more to me than my lunch. I want you to have what I never had.' Hank Aaron said that every time he thought about that fifty-cent piece that his father put on the table every day, he thought how much that fifty cents meant to his father. It conveyed to him how much his schooling meant to his father."[3]

Without education Hank still would have been a great baseball player. However, he may not have been the man of character that he was without his father's lesson on education. So many who achieve great fame and fortune are not well rounded and thus dilute the influence they might have had.

## REASONS FOR EDUCATION

Education is simply defined as the imparting and acquiring of knowledge. What good is it to know your life mission if you don't have the knowledge to accomplish it? Proverbs reminds us, "A wise man will hear, and will increase learning" (Proverbs 1:5). We live in the greatest information age in history. We can find out almost anything about any subject within minutes with the help of technology. There are multiple reasons to gain an education, but I'll mention just two.

## 1. EDUCATION INCREASES OUR LEADERSHIP ABILITY

One of my favorite things to do every week is to read in the *Church News* about the newly called stake, mission, and temple presidents.

I enjoy seeing what they do for an occupation, and the variety is impressive. The one thing they have in common, however, is that as a group they are highly educated. Over the years I have been in meetings where various names were considered for callings. Never once in all these years have I heard anyone mention how much formal education the person being considered had. And yet, it is remarkable how much education Church leaders do have. I grew up in a small town in Southeast Texas. As is typical of small towns, the population as a whole is not considered highly educated. The vast majority of those who graduate from the local high school do not graduate from college. Twenty-two men have served as bishops of the four wards in that small city during the past thirty-five years. Of those who served, one had two years of college, three had bachelor's degrees, seven had master's degrees, and the other eleven had advanced professional degrees.

The Lord often uses highly educated people with strong testimonies to fill leadership positions in our complex society. Surely, that is in part to elevate leaders who can teach the gospel with their hearts and their minds. Being educated is not always about the number of degrees one holds. Joseph Smith and Brigham Young were two of the most learned people of their day, yet their education did not come from major universities. President Hinckley did not hold advanced degrees, but he was well educated.

The same thing holds true for leadership in our cities, states, and countries. Those with educated minds can be a great influence for good when they combine that education with gospel principles. No matter what your mission is in life, it most likely will require you to lead others, because you are the specialist. When you know how to lead, life gets much easier. Elder Sterling W. Sill related this story:

> Everything is easy when you know how. An interesting story is told of Ralph Waldo Emerson trying to get a calf into the barn. This particular calf had not been fully persuaded that he should do what Mr. Emerson wanted him to do. Mr. Emerson lacked something in know-how so far as calves were concerned. The great scholar from Concord took his logical position at the calf's rear and forcibly tried to propel the calf into the barn. The harder Mr. Emerson pushed, the more firmly the calf braced

himself to resist. Mr. Emerson pushed and puffed and said some uncomplimentary things about calves, but the calf held the line. The struggle left Mr. Emerson with exactly no ground gained. Then an Irish servant girl came by, and seeing the predicament offered a helping hand. She put one finger of that hand into the calf's mouth and started for the barn. The calf, enticed by this maternal imitation, went along enthusiastically. As Mr. Emerson wiped the perspiration from his steaming, scholarly brow and proceeded to cleanse his hands of their bovine smell, he was heard to mutter to himself, "I like people who can do things." A good question for us to ask ourselves about our leadership is, "Can we get the calf into the barn?"[4]

Joseph Smith said, "A man is saved no faster than he gets knowledge, for if he does not get knowledge, he will be brought into captivity by some evil power in the other world, as evil spirits will have more knowledge, and consequently more power than many men who are on the earth. Hence it needs revelation to assist us, and give us knowledge of the things of God."[5]

Your Father in Heaven sent you to earth with a divine mission. The adversary will do everything he can to sabotage that mission. If you don't have more knowledge than those with evil power, you will fail.

## 2. THE LORD COMMANDED IT AND SAID IT WAS GOOD

Throughout the scriptures, the Lord urges his people to become educated. Those with great missions to perform share a thirst for knowledge. For example, Abraham had a great mission to perform and is known as the "father of the faithful" (Doctrine and Covenants 138:41). He desired "also to be one who possessed great knowledge" (Abraham 1:2). Do you desire great knowledge? Those sent to earth in the last days were saved for a great purpose. Maybe that is why the message to seek knowledge and wisdom seems to be more urgent in latter-day scripture. Consider the following:

•   "[S]eek learning, even by study and also by faith. (Doctrine and Covenants 88:118)

- "[S]tudy and learn, and become acquainted with all good books, and with languages, tongues, and people. (Doctrine and Covenants 90:15)

- "[O]btain a knowledge of history, and of countries, and of kingdoms, of laws of God and man, and all this for the salvation of Zion. (Doctrine and Covenants 93:53)

- "And if a person gains more knowledge and intelligence in this life through his diligence and obedience than another, he will have so much the advantage in the world to come." (Doctrine and Covenants 130:19)

- "It is impossible for a man to be saved in ignorance." (Doctrine and Covenants 131:6)

Great knowledge and education, however, can be poison if not sought by faith. Often there is an increased correlation between pride and learning. "O the vainness, and the frailties, and the foolishness of men! When they are learned they think they are wise, and they hearken not unto the counsel of God, for they set it aside, supposing they know of themselves, wherefore, their wisdom is foolishness and it profiteth them not. And they shall perish" (2 Nephi 9:28). Make sure the knowledge you seek is related to your divine mission and that the Lord is involved. The previous warning is followed by, "But to be learned is good if they hearken unto the counsels of God" (2 Nephi 9:29).

We are told that the "glory of God is intelligence" (Doctrine and Covenants 93:36). That being the case, then what is the glory of man? Elder Mark E. Petersen taught, "We believe also that the glory of man is likewise intelligence. With this in mind, we are strong advocates of education."[6]

Who do you want to associate with in the next life? Your pursuit of knowledge in this life is highly correlated with those people who will make up your companions in the next. Brigham Young explained, "We need constant instruction, and our great heavenly Teacher requires of us to be diligent pupils in his school, that we may in time reach his glorified presence. If we will not lay to heart the rules of education which our Teacher gives us to study, and continue to advance from one branch of learning to another, we never can be scholars of the first class and become endowed with the science, power, excellency, brightness and glory of the heavenly hosts; and unless we are educated as they are, we cannot associate with them."[7]

# ONE MAJOR GOAL PER YEAR

Joseph Smith did not just have the role of a great prophet and teacher. He was also a mayor, general, candidate for president of the United States, record keeper, husband, father, and more. Each of these responsibilities required a different skill set. Your mission will most likely be multi-faceted.

My friend Phil taught me this lesson. When he and his family moved from their home, a worker from the moving company looked over their possessions and asked, "Who is this guy?" Phil had built the beautiful log cabin home they were leaving from the bottom up, with no previous building experience. He had even purchased the portable sawmill and milled his own logs for the home. In the packing boxes were scuba gear, tennis racquets, art and carving supplies, skis, books written in Greek, and many other items that indicated the wide variety of interests and talents of the owner.

"How can one man have so many talents?" the mover asked. Phil's wife explained that her husband had a tradition. At the beginning of every year, he picked a talent or hobby to work on. During the next twelve months, he concentrated and devoted time to that talent. He read about it, took classes, and practiced it until he became proficient. When the year was over, he picked up a new talent or hobby. But, he did not let his previously developed talents die. He continued to use the knowledge acquired in the past.

I first met Phil at a convention during which he played a beautiful and difficult classical piano piece. When he finished, someone requested another song. He said he was sorry, but he didn't know how to play the piano. There was puzzled silence after his comment. The song he had just played was something he had worked on the entire year, and he now felt that he was ready to take piano lessons. I watched him in a tennis match against a man previously state-ranked in high school.

Phil had taken tennis lessons, studied techniques, and practiced the sport for a year. He won the match easily that day.

What a powerful idea to apply to education; concentrate on something for an entire year and in twenty years you could be an expert in twenty fields. The scriptures state that, "A wise man will hear, and will increase learning" (Proverbs 1:5). I know that Phil has inspired hundreds of people with his drive to be educated in multiple areas of life. He certainly inspired me, and I have tried to do a similar thing over the years because of his example. Perhaps that is his life mission.

President Howard W. Hunter said, "I am reminded of what Abraham Lincoln said when he sat on the sidelines for a long time, losing election after election and struggling to make a professional contribution. He said simply, 'I will prepare, and perhaps my chance will come.' He lived long enough to learn what everyone learns—that chance always favors the prepared life."[8] With that preparation, Abraham Lincoln saved our nation from chaos. He fulfilled his mission because he was prepared. Do you have the knowledge that prepares you to fulfill the assignment the Lord gave you? If you do not have it yet, do you have a plan to obtain it?

Notes

1. Dallin H. Oaks, "Getting to Know China," BYU devotional address, March 12, 1991.
2. R. Lanier Britsch, *From the East: The History of the Latter-day Saints in Asia*, 1851–1996, 303.
3. Thomas S. Monson, *Be Your Best Self*, 173.
4. Sterling W. Sill, *Leadership*, 60–61.
5. Joseph Smith, *History of the Church*, 4:588.
6. Mark E. Petersen, "Hear Ye Him," *Ensign*, November 1975, 63.
7. Brigham Young, *Journal of Discourses*, 10:266.
8. Howard W. Hunter, "Bind on Thy Sandals," *Ensign*, May 1978, 34.

# CHAPTER 11

# ESTABLISH A
# SPECIFIC PLAN

*Plan your work; work your plan.*

—Stephen R. Covey

When my wife was a stake Young Women president, I was astounded at the amount of planning that went into the annual girls' camp. Long before the actual event, the leaders began meeting to choose a theme and formulate a plan. My wife patiently tried to explain to me the many factors involved, such as dates, location, transportation, food, activities, special programs, workshops, speakers, priesthood support, age-group skill requirements, t-shirts, housing, hikes, level-leader training, first-aid specialists, lifeguards, games, duty rosters, set-up, clean-up, testimony meetings and so on. Seldom do you see a stake girls' camp that has not been planned out in great detail. And seldom do you witness a testimony meeting more transforming and moving than at an LDS girls' camp.

Growing up in a small Texas town, I didn't know what it was like to have a ward with a surplus of leaders to go around. Even though most boys my age went to Mutual every Wednesday night, we seldom had a leader with us. We were on our own to play games and goof off. It was fun, but all of the boys my age barely made it past the Tenderfoot rank in the Boy Scouts program. Most of us probably weren't even aware there were ranks in scouts. Not one boy had a scout shirt, much less a full uniform. We didn't even know what one looked like. Fancy clothes belonged to another world. (Some of my cousins were barefoot when they passed the sacrament.)

Most of our campouts involved a bunch of cousins and friends, with no adult supervision. These campouts were quite different from the typical girls' camp of today. This was the sum total of our planning: "Hey, let's go camping Friday night." I'm not sure why that always sounded fun, because that was never the case. At night we lay on the ground in the heat and humidity of summer, or freezing in winter with sticks or pine needles poking us. Every summer we endured swarming mosquitoes that were not dissuaded by our constant swatting. We had no tents and no sleeping bags. Sometimes I remembered to bring a sheet or a blanket, depending on the season. Occasionally, I brought a pillow, but not often. Little wonder that today I don't like to go camping.

When I became a scout leader, I understood the value of planning ahead; still, no one would mistake me for a member of the girls' camp committee. About a week before the campout, I would gather the young men and say something like this: "Okay, boys, we are going on a week-long campout starting next Monday. Everyone meet at the Church at 8:00 AM. We are going to try to find a place to go rock climbing, white water rafting, mountain biking, and skeet shooting. If any of you have any ideas of places we could go, please see me afterwards. Now this is very important. Be sure to bring everything you need. Does anyone have any questions? Okay, then, we'll see you on Monday morning, and be sure not to forget anything. Also, don't be late. Oh yeah, if anyone has a truck, please bring it."

Many of us plan our lives the way I planned my campouts. Maybe that is why some are not having all that much fun. However, if you can learn the Lord's will for you and then make a detailed plan of how to achieve it, you are going to have a wonderful time, although there will still be mosquitoes.

# What Is the Plan?

The dictionary defines a *plan* as a scheme or method of acting, doing, proceeding, making, or developing in advance. Over the years I have talked to hundreds of young people about their futures. Many have no plan at all for where they are going or how they will get there. Occasionally, however, I talk to Nathan or Allen, two of my former institute students. They were unusual because they both had detailed plans. They were about the same age and were first cousins.

Nathan told me before his mission that he wanted to be a medical doctor. I had heard students voice that ambition before. Many young people say the same thing until they take organic chemistry; then their plans change in the amount of time it takes to register for ballroom dance. Nathan was pretty specific; he wanted to be a medical researcher in the field of cancer. I was impressed that he had thought about his career in such detail, but I doubted he would accomplish what he said he would do because he was still in his teens. Years passed, and I was serving in the San Antonio Mission presidency. As part of my responsibilities, I spoke at a stake conference in our mission. As I was sitting on the stand waiting for the meeting to start, I looked at the printed program and saw a familiar name—it was Nathan. I leaned over and asked a stake leader if he knew what Nathan did for a living. "Yes, he's a medical doctor." I asked if he knew Nathan's specialty. "He's a cancer researcher."

The next year, I was invited to speak to a Relief Society group in an area several hundred miles from where I live. I accepted the invitation because it came from a sister who said I knew her bishop. His name was Allen, and he had been one of my institute students. My mind went back several years to a conversation I had with Allen. I had asked him what he wanted to do for a career, and he told me that he wanted to be a biomedical engineer and work on artificial body parts. I remember thinking, "Where in the world did he come up with that idea? I have never met anyone who did that." The night I spoke to the Relief Society group, I saw Allen for the first time in many years. I asked him what he was doing for a living. He told me that he was a biomedical engineer working with artificial body parts.

Nathan and Allen had learned some valuable lessons very early in life. Not only had they envisioned what they were going to do for occupations and had set goals to make it happen, but they had also developed plans to accomplish those goals. The plans included many elements, such as where to go to college, what classes were needed to prepare for their specialties, and how to pay for school. Those parts and many others had been formulated into a big-picture plan to reach their goals. Elder Sterling W. Sill said, "We have a great power in our ability to plan. No one generates more power than the planner, the thinker, the organizer, the doer. He is the one who draws the blueprint for success. He is the one who builds the roadway on which every accomplishment will travel."[1]

More typical is the story I heard in a sacrament meeting in January 2000. One of our speakers was Dwayne. He mentioned that he had received a call recently from a childhood friend, who asked, "Hey, Dwayne, do you remember when we were teenagers, and we wrote out goals for what we would be doing in the year 2000?" Dwayne replied, "No, but I have a feeling that I'm going to be reminded." His friend had held on to the list over the years, and he read what Dwayne had written: "In the year 2000 I will be a medical doctor living in a big house with seven children." I'll never forget what Dwayne said next: "Well, here I am in the year 2000. I'm a 34-year old pastry chef and not married. But I do work near doctors and their big homes, and they buy my pastries."

Dwayne's story reminds us that our dreams and goals don't always turn out the way we envisioned them in our youth. His goals were not realized, but not for lack of intellectual ability or financial resources. Life has a way of changing the dreams of those who are not totally committed and do not have a specific plan. President Spencer W. Kimball said, "Failure to plan brings barrenness and sterility. Fate brushes man with its wings, but we make our own fate largely. Karl G. Maeser gave us this thought-provoking statement of those who do not make that fate happen: 'And the books will be opened and my guardian angel will stand by me and as he opens the book he will say, 'Look,' and I will look and say: 'How beautiful.' And the angel will say, 'That is what you could have been, and then he will turn the leaf and say, 'This is what you have been.'"[2]

If Dwayne wanted to be a doctor, he needed a plan just like

Nathan's. Dwayne would have begun in high school, studying hard to qualify himself for a good college. In college, the plan would include taking pre-med classes and maintaining a high grade point average, studying for the medical school admission test and applying to medical schools.

## Planning Things Out

On a trip from Austin, Texas, to Virginia to run an Especially for Youth session, Wendy and I had a layover in Chicago's O'Hare Airport. As the plane descended into Chicago, I looked out my window and saw the magnificent Sears Tower right below me. For years it was the tallest building in the world at 110 stories and 1,454 feet. Its construction had not been haphazard or hasty. The Savior gave instructions to those who are sent to earth to build towers of another sort: "For which of you, intending to build a tower, sitteth not down first, and counteth the cost, whether he have sufficient to finish it?" (Luke 14:28)

When the Savior gave that counsel, he was speaking to other than just the builders of earthly towers. He was talking to you. It is foolish to believe that you can accomplish what you were sent to do without a specific, detailed plan. At some point, someone had a vision of the Sears Tower. But having a vision of a building does not get the job done. The visionary likely said, "I have a goal to build the tallest building in the world." However, as important as goals are, they do not get skyscrapers built. A blueprint is needed.

The blueprint for a building like the Sears Tower consists of many pages of minute detail. No builder would think of starting a tower or even a house without a detailed set of blueprints for every phase of the building. These plans ultimately tell the builder everything needed to complete the building. It is a guide for items to be purchased, such as cement, I-beams, windows, doors, and air conditioning units. It also guides the builder to the precise spot, down to the square inch, where each item will be placed in the building.

Builders keep their plans in front of them at all times. When problems arise, they don't throw out the blueprints; they look at them more closely to make sure they are following the plan.

# PLAN HOW YOU WILL
# ACCOMPLISH YOUR GOALS

A ship's captain does not head out to sea without a compass and a plan for where he will take his ship. Neither should you say, "You know, I've never really thought about where I'm going. I guess I will cross that bridge when I come to it." Mormon described this aimless person when he said, "But now, behold, they are led about by Satan, even as chaff is driven before the wind, or as a vessel is tossed about upon the waves, without sail or anchor, or without anything wherewith to steer her; and even as she is, so are they" (Mormon 5:18). Every great accomplishment—whether building a cathedral, creating a work of art, designing a computer, sending a man to the Moon, or achieving a mission—takes a detailed plan of action.

Your Heavenly Father has a plan for all of his children to return to him. It is called the *plan* of salvation. The plan is a detailed written program, recorded in scripture. King Benjamin explained the necessity of having such a blueprint for earth life. Speaking of the brass plates, where the plan was kept in Lehi's day, he recorded, "I say unto you, my sons, were it not for these things, which have been kept and preserved by the hand of God, that we might read and understand of his mysteries, and have his commandments always before our eyes, that *even our fathers would have dwindled in unbelief, and we should have been like unto our brethren, the Lamanites*, who know nothing concerning these things, or even do not believe them when they are taught them" (Mosiah 1:5, emphasis added). King Benjamin is referring to Lehi, Nephi, Jacob, Enos, and Mosiah when he says "our fathers." He is saying that they would have stumbled like the Lamanites without the written plan to guide them.

With this in mind, it becomes obvious why Nephi had to get the brass plates at all cost before his family went off to a new life in a promised land. They were the blueprints for how to return to Heavenly Father, the whole purpose of this earth life. Without the plan, all would be lost. That is why it was better that "one man should perish than that a nation should dwindle and perish in unbelief" (1 Nephi 4:13). These inspired leaders knew that the written plan was essential to bring people to Christ. King Lamoni, who was converted by Ammon, realized this and said, "And the great God has had mercy on us, and made these things known unto us that we might not perish; yea, and he has made these things known unto us beforehand, because he loveth our souls as well as he loveth our children; therefore, in his mercy he doth visit us by his angels, that the *plan of salvation might be made known unto us as well as unto future generations*" (Alma 24:14, emphasis added).

Heavenly Father not only has an overall plan for all of his children, but also an individual plan for you. Elder Neal A. Maxwell shared what you must do to realize that plan. He said, "It is only by yielding to God that we can begin to realize His will for us. And if we truly trust God, why not yield to His loving omniscience? After all, He knows us and our possibilities much better than do we."[3]

But where do you go to learn his will for you? The Lord has provided many tools:

- **Scriptures:** Brigham Young said they "are like a lighthouse in the ocean or a fingerpost which points out the road we should travel."[4] You should read them with the specific intent to discover ideas that will help you plan the course of your life.

- **Teachings of the living prophets:** There are certain guidelines that we all need to follow regardless of our individual missions. President Harold B. Lee spoke of this when he said, "If you want to know what the Lord has for this people at the present time, I would admonish you to get and read the discourses that have been delivered at this conference."[5]

- **Patriarchal blessings:** Remember President Thomas S. Monson's statement: "The same Lord who provided a Liahona for Lehi provides for *you* and for me today a rare and valuable gift to give *direction to our lives*, to mark the hazards to our safety, and to *chart the way*, even safe passage—-not to a promised land, but *to our heavenly home*. The gift to which I refer is known as your patriarchal blessing."[6]

- **Inspiration gained by prayer and pondering:** Lorenzo Snow said that God "has conferred upon us His Holy Spirit, which is an unerring guide, standing, as an angel of God, at our side, telling us what to do, and affording us strength and succor when adverse circumstances arise in our way."[7]

If you will use these four resources to develop your blueprint, you will surely begin to know the Lord's will for you. Elder Sterling W. Sill told of an experience he had with a blueprint:

Recently I was in the office of a building contractor who was erecting a multimillion-dollar building. He had spread out before him a set of drawings that he called a blueprint. And I was impressed with this idea that any builder can erect the most magnificent building that the greatest architect can conceive, if he just knows how to follow the blueprint. And then I tried unsuccessfully to think of any idea in the world more important. The best sculptor is the one who can most accurately reproduce in marble the image that he sees before him. The good cook follows the recipe. The pharmacist can utilize the many years of training of the most famous doctors from the best medical schools, if he just knows how to follow a prescription. Someone has said that science is just a collection of successful formulas.[8]

## SET DEADLINES

After your plans are formulated, attach deadlines to them. Each step needs to be broken down and every step needs its own deadline. The final goal is reached when all of the separate deadlines have been met.

My wife and I were out driving and saw a large partially finished building. On one of the cement walls I saw a banner with a familiar red and white bull's-eye logo and a grand opening date. A company had seen this piece of land for sale and made a goal to build a store on the site. Plans were formulated to purchase the land, obtain the necessary permits, and complete the preliminary work. Ultimately, after multiple necessary steps, a detailed blueprint was drawn up for the newest Target store. I'm sure that along the way several deadlines were met until the planners felt comfortable hanging the banner announcing the completion date.

Do deadlines work? Just drive by a post office at midnight on April 15. The Internal Revenue Service sets the deadline, and millions of Americans answer the call. Without the deadline, what percentage of the taxes would be paid?

Work on an overall plan to accomplish your life mission. Then break that plan down in enough detail that you know what must be done every year and eventually every month and every day. Stephen R. Covey gave this valuable advice: "Plan your week; plan each day. Plan where you want to spend your time and with whom, doing what. Planning is faith. Planning is setting goals and a program to achieve them. Planning is thinking. Planning is serving 'with your mind.' Half an hour in daily, careful planning will double or triple the effectiveness of your ten hours of work. Planning requires mental discipline, patience, and a lot of practice. Do not become discouraged in your initial struggling effort to develop the planning skill. Stay with it in faith. . . . Plan your work; work your plan . . ."[9]

Everything you see around you started with a plan. There is a blueprint for every accomplishment. What is your plan? The last thing to remember in this process was expressed by Elder L. Tom Perry who said, "You must plan your day as guided by the Spirit of the Lord."[10]

------

Notes

1. Sterling W. Sill, *Principles, Promises, and Powers*, 27.
2. Spencer W. Kimball, "Seagull Monument," in Conference Report, October 1970, 72.
3. Neal A. Maxwell, "Willing to Submit," *Ensign*, May 1985, 72.
4. Brigham Young, *Journal of Discourses*, 8:129.
5. Harold B. Lee, "Stand Ye in Holy Places," *Ensign*, July 1973, 121.
6. Thomas S. Monson, "A Provident Plan—A Precious Promise," *Ensign*, November 1986, 62, emphasis added.
7. Brigham Young, *Journal of Discourses*, 20:191.
8. Sterling W. Sill, in Conference Report, April 1962, 13–14.
9. Stephen R. Covey, *Spiritual Roots of Human Relations*, 279.
10. L. Tom Perry, "Fatherhood, an Eternal Calling," *Ensign*, May 2004, 69.

# CHAPTER 12

# WORK HARD

*Put your shoulder to the wheel!*

—*Hymns*, no. 252

A story is told of a man named Joe who refused to work. He sat on the porch every day in his rocking chair and did nothing. Joe was living proof of Proverbs 23:21: "Drowsiness shall clothe a man with rags." The only way Joe could eat was if the home teachers, bishop, or ward members brought him food. One day the frustrated bishop stopped by and told Joe that if he wasn't going to work then he might as well go to the cemetery and wait to die. Joe got up from his rocker, climbed into the back of the bishop's wagon and lay down for the trip to the cemetery. En route they passed another ward member who asked where they were going. The bishop said he was tired of feeding Joe and was taking him to the cemetery to die. The ward member said, "I have some corn that he can have."

Joe rose up back of the wagon and asked, "Is it shucked?"

"No, it's still in the husks."

Joe lay back down and said, "Drive on, Bishop."

I contrast the story of Joe with an experience my wife and I had with Gabe. We have a forty-acre weekend ranch with ten longhorn cattle that roam the land. We go out quite often to check on the cows, and occasionally, we have to buy extra hay to supplement their range diet. Our feed supplier, Gabe, doesn't have an advanced degree, and he doesn't make a lot of money to support his large family, but he is cheerful about the work he does and goes about it efficiently. He is tall,

107

slender, and strong, able to heft a bail of hay in each bare hand and stack it without breaking stride.

I doubt Gabe's life mission is to feed our longhorns, but I do know he is a great example of a hard worker. On one drive home after having hay delivered, Wendy asked me how I wanted to be remembered after I was gone. I thought of Gabe and his work ethic, spending his days cutting, bailing, stacking, loading, and delivering hay. He does it year round in the Texas heat and humidity. It is a grueling job, yet he loves it. I told my wife that I wanted to be known as a hard worker like Gabe. Life missions will take hard work to achieve. The Lord is not going to give you a lazy man's mission.

Many of us have big plans and goals in life. For example, we are going to climb Mount Everest while carving a nativity set out of olive wood on the way up. When we get back from that trip we will learn to play the piano, guitar, trombone, and harp, and perform as a one-man band at the ward talent show. Then we'll build a log cabin from scratch and . . .

Most of us talk a good line during the dreaming phase. Some of us even plan in detail how we will accomplish our dreams. But when the backbreaking hard work comes, many of our dreams quickly fade. Sometimes we even feel we're making progress and working hard by buying a book about Mount Everest instead of climbing it. But then, even the book sits unread on the shelf.

Grand ideas dance through our heads when we're closing our eyes at night. Then the alarm goes off the next morning, and we push the snooze button. Too many of us would rather watch TV specials about great people than to be great ourselves. We could earn ourselves this epitaph: "He lived in the world of going-to do but died with nothing done."

To attain an established goal, diligent, hard work must follow. What good is a ceremonial ground breaking if no one shows up the next day with a backhoe? This is the most difficult, yet most important part of the process. The scriptures allude to this step by saying, "But be ye doers of the word, and not hearers only, deceiving your own selves" (James 1:22).

All achievers in life must work to make things happen. Elder F. David Stanley said, "Great athletes are hard workers. Points, rebounds, assists, tackles, goals, and home runs are all the result of long hours of painstaking practice and hard work. The bulk of that practice will always be on your own, away from the coach. Victory is brought to pass by one's personal diligence and commitment to hard work. The view of a champion, and the glory that surrounds him, must never be overshadowed by the long process of becoming one. There is a time of preparation and a time of victory. The second mile of hard work is what makes the difference between the exhilaration of achievement and the acceptance of mediocrity."[1]

## CAPACITY TO WORK

When I first began college, I struggled financially. Jobs were difficult to find in Idaho until potato season came along. Two of my friends and I were excited when we got a job in a potato cellar. We mistakenly thought it would be an easy way to make money. All we had to do was use a large pitchfork to scoop potatoes to a conveyor belt. Each scoop weighed only about twenty-five pounds—not heavy at all. The first day on the job, I found that the twenty-five pounds began to feel like fifty pounds after the first thirty minutes. By the end of the first hour, it felt like each scoop weighed at least seventy-five pounds, with the weight increasing with each raise of the shovel. One of my roommates quit that first day. He said he didn't need money that badly. That night, I was so exhausted and sore that I fell into bed.

The next day after classes, two of us went back to work. My friend quit before the day was over, and I wanted badly to join him, but I had to have the money. With each scoop, I wanted to walk out the door, but I didn't quit. What kept me going? The man on the other side of the conveyor belt from me was probably seventy years old but worked like a machine. Every time I wanted to quit, I looked at the old man and kept going because I was not going to let him beat me.

I learned something from that experience. If you don't quit, your capacity increases. I got so good at scooping potatoes that I got a raise—not in salary but in muscle mass. As I grew stronger, my employer put me at the end of the line where I took the 100-pound sacks and dragged them over against the wall. That job was extremely difficult, but I learned another valuable lesson. President Spencer W. Kimball summed up the lesson I learned: "Working develops the capacity to work. One of the numerous rewards in girding ourselves to do hard things is in the creation of a capacity for doing of the still harder things."[2]

Accomplishing anything of lasting value in life is going to take work, and lots of it. My wife and I had an opportunity to visit Rome. During our stay, we toured Vatican City, the world headquarters of the Catholic Church, and St. Peter's Basilica. According to Catholic tradition, this magnificent building holds the tomb of the Apostle Peter beneath the altar. To many, this building is the greatest of its age. Architects and architectural historians have called it the greatest of all churches of Christendom.

As I entered the building, its grandeur was stunning. I wondered how anyone could envision such a creation; much less make it a reality. The centerpiece of this magnificent edifice is its huge central dome—the work of Michelangelo. Not only was he the architect of St. Peter's Basilica, he also painted the ceiling of its Sistine Chapel with scenes from Genesis. And he painted the Last Judgment on the altar wall. As a sculptor, his works include *The Pieta and David*, both created before he was thirty years old. He was also a poet. And none of it came easily to him. He said, "If people knew how hard I have had to work to gain my mastery, it would not seem wonderful at all."[3]

Most people are not willing to pay the price that Michelangelo paid. We mortals have a problem. President Gordon B. Hinckley described it: "I believe in the gospel of work. . . . We are all inherently lazy. We would rather play than work. We would rather loaf than work. . . . But it is work that spells the difference in the life of a man or woman."[4]

## Everyone Is Busy

Some people think because they are busy, they are accomplishing great things. Just keeping busy is not what you were sent here to do. All of us can account for our time and in most cases consider ourselves hard workers. Let's take a look at the schedule of an imaginary, yet typical, college student:

- Got up at 8:45 AM
- Went to 9:00 AM class
- Walked to the institute and hung out for a couple of hours
- Lunch

- Went to two more classes
- Studied a little at the library
- Took short nap because I stayed up too late
- Jogged and took a shower
- Watched TV
- Called parents to tell them how hard college was
- Went to friend's house and watched a movie
- Hung out after the movie
- Surfed the internet
- Played computer games
- Stayed up working on overdue paper until 2:00 AM
- Too tired to go to class the next morning

The schedule of this imaginary student may not be too different from many of your own days. The hours are filled, but the day is empty of substance. Those close to President Hinckley knew him as a tireless worker. He would wear out far younger people during his many travels. But he wasn't merely "busy." He was busy accomplishing the mission he was sent to do. Some of us probably think we are busier than President Hinckley was since we stay up until 2 AM doing something. The test, however, is what we accomplish during the time we are busy and what we leave behind. Here are a few of the things President Hinckley left behind as evidences of his handiwork. Many of the following occurred after he was sustained as prophet at age eighty-five:

- Built his own home
- Gave thousands of talks
- Wrote multiple magazine articles
- Participated in hundreds of media interviews
- Wrote hundreds of pamphlets and scripts
- Changed the image of the Church worldwide
- Produced movies, filmstrips, and other teaching aids
- Had the Nauvoo Temple rebuilt
- Traveled more than any other Church leader in history
- Directed the transition of Ricks College to BYU–Idaho
- Awarded the Presidential Medal of Freedom
- Distributed Church materials to libraries in North America
- Was responsible for the building of most of the world's temples

- Directed the design and construction of the Conference Center
- Set up the Perpetual Education Fund
- Authored several best-selling books
- Released "The Family: A Proclamation to the World"
- Established new visitors' centers
- Created temple films
- Had the Tabernacle refurbished
- Had Cove Fort restored
- Released new Handbook of Instructions
- Had Hotel Utah restored

President Hinckley left a legacy like few in history have because he understood his mission. He believed the words of Thomas Jefferson: "I'm a great believer in luck, and I find the harder I work the more I have of it."[5] But just knowing his mission does not explain how he did it. Once he realized his mission and made his plan, he worked night and day to make it happen. In the process, he left things behind for everyone to benefit from. If you were to die today, what would you leave behind? What do you wish you were leaving behind? Many of us spend our time wishing for things when we *could have* those things if we spent our time working instead of wishing.

During the Industrial Revolution in the late Nineteenth Century, the Bethlehem Steel Corporation became the largest independent steel producer in the world under the leadership of its president Charles M. Schwab. He was responsible for the development of the H-beam, a precursor to today's I-beam. This product revolutionized building construction and made modern skyscrapers possible. Although he was extremely successful, Schwab never stopped looking for ways to improve productivity both in his steel mills and in his life. Ivy Lee, a public relations consultant and efficiency guru, called on Schwab one day and offered him an idea to improve productivity. Lee told Schwab that he could teach him a management system in twenty minutes that would allow him and his executives to accomplish 50 percent more work without having to put in longer hours.

Schwab said he would pay anything Lee asked if the idea would do what he claimed. Lee supposedly pulled out a small blank card and explained his system. Each night, Schwab was to list the ten (some accounts say six) of the most important things that needed to be accomplished the next day, ranking them in order of urgency. Then he told Schwab to put the sheet in his pocket and start working on the list the first thing in the morning. During the day he was to look at the to-do list several times, working down the list in order. The idea was to get number one accomplished before moving on to number two.

Lee reportedly told Schwab to try it himself first and then get his executives to try it. Only then was Schwab to send Lee a check for what he thought the plan was worth. The entire interview reportedly lasted about twenty minutes. Schwab tried the method himself and then had his people at Bethlehem Steel try it. What happened next has been widely reported. Schwab sent Ivy Lee a check for $25,000 for the idea that dramatically increased production for the company. Today that simple idea is still widely used in the business world and touted by time-management experts.

Thomas Edison was a man known for getting things done. He has been called history's greatest inventor. He had a mission to light the world and did just that. Edison held 1,093 patents, a world record. It is reported that before Edison succeeded in making the electric light, he conducted thousands of experiments. During this period he was often asked, "Have you found it yet?" and he would reply, "No, but I have found a lot of ways that won't work." He attributed the secret of his success to hard work. Here are some of his words on the subject:

- I never did anything worth doing by accident, nor did any of my inventions come by accident; they came by work.
- Many of life's failures are people who did not realize how close they were to success when they gave up.
- Show me a thoroughly satisfied man and I will show you a failure.
- There is no substitute for hard work.
- Opportunity is missed by most people because it is dressed in overalls and looks like work.
- The first requisite for success is the ability to apply your physical and mental energies to one problem incessantly without growing weary.
- Genius is one percent inspiration and ninety-nine percent perspiration.[6]

We sing a hymn in the Church about the need for workers to build up the kingdom in the last days. As you read the words, ask yourself what part you are to play in this great work.

### Put Your Shoulder to the Wheel

The world has need of willing men
Who wear the worker's seal.
Come, help the good work move along;
Put your shoulder to the wheel.

*Chorus:*
Put your shoulder to the wheel; push along,
Do your duty with a heart full of song,
We all have work; let no one shirk.
Put your shoulder to the wheel.

The Church has need of helping hands,
And hearts that know and feel.
The work to do is here for you;
Put your shoulder to the wheel.

Then don't stand idly looking on;
The fight with sin is real.
It will be long but must go on;
Put your shoulder to the wheel.

Then work and watch and fight and pray
With all your might and zeal.
Push ev'ry worthy work along;
Put your shoulder to the wheel.[7]

Nothing gets done until someone is willing to put his shoulder to the wheel. However, it is possible to be a hard worker and still not accomplish anything of value. Fill your days with meaningful work that moves your mission forward. You are looking for victory the Lord's way, and "All victory and glory is brought to pass unto you through your diligence, faithfulness, and prayers of faith" (Doctrine and Covenants 130:36).

---

Notes

1. F. David Stanley, "The Principle of Work," *Ensign*, May 1993, 44.
2. Spencer W. and Edward L. Kimball, *Teachings of Spencer W. Kimball*, 362.
3. Michelangelo, quotations.com.
4. Gordon B. Hinckley, "Articles of Belief," Bonneville International Management Seminar, February 10, 1991.
5. Thomas Jefferson, quotationspage.com.
6. Thomas Edison, quotations.about.com.
7. "Put Your Shoulder to the Wheel," *Hymns*, no. 252.

# CHAPTER 13

❦

# Gain the Desire
# And Determination
# Needed to Suceed

*Many of life's failures are men who did not realize
how close they were to success when they gave up.*

—Thomas Edison

As a stake visitor to a Deacon's Quorum one Sunday, I was taught a powerful lesson about desire. It was fast Sunday and the teacher built the lesson on one of the beatitudes from Jesus' Sermon on the Mount: "Blessed are they which do hunger and thirst after righteousness: for they shall be filled" (Matthew 5:6). Toward the end of class, the boys became a little restless as stomachs grumbled. But all of them were snapped back to attention when the teacher pulled out a large plastic bowl and popped off the lid. The aroma of freshly baked chocolate chip cookies wafted across the room. I wanted one of those cookies as badly as they did. At the teacher's direction, they passed the bowl around. Their assignment was to look and inhale, but not touch. The boys exercised admirable restraint, in anticipation of being rewarded at the end of class.

Their teacher closed the lesson by challenging the deacons to have righteous desires, as in the beatitude. Then he called on someone to offer the closing prayer. After the "amen," he put the lid back on the container and started to walk out of the room. "But what about the cookies?" the boys wanted to know. The teacher gently reminded them that it was fast Sunday and he could not give them treats. Then he delivered the powerful lesson: "When you have a desire for righteousness like you do for these cookies right now, you will get it." He turned and walked away with all of his cookies.

This teacher may have borrowed his object lesson from a story told of Socrates. Elder Royden G. Derrick retold it in general conference: "A young man approached Socrates and asked him to be his tutor and to teach him what he knew. Socrates took the young man to the seaside and out into the water. Then he pushed his head under the water for almost too long. The young man struggled, came up gasping for air, and demanded the meaning of such an unwarranted action. The great Socrates responded, 'When you want to learn as badly as you want a breath of air, only then can I teach you what you want to know.'"[1]

Fulfilling a life mission begins with a desire to learn what it is and how it can be accomplished. Righteous desires bring tremendous blessings from the Lord, who said, "And then shall ye know, or by this shall you know, all things whatsoever you desire of me, which are pertaining unto things of righteousness, in faith believing in me that you shall receive" (Doctrine and Covenants 11:14).

Although some dictionaries define a wish and a desire synonymously, I have learned over the years that wishing for something and really desiring something are quite different. For example, I really wish I could play the piano. A couple of times I have even tried to learn how to play. I have spent a grand total of four hours trying to master this skill. For some reason, I still cannot play the piano, but I *wish* I could. If someone could sell me the talent I would definitely *try* to come up with the money. But learning to play the piano is not for sale. If I don't have the desire, I will never play the piano. How badly do I wish I could play the piano? Enough to practice two hours per day? No. One hour per day? No. Thirty minutes? Fifteen? Obviously not. But I sure do wish I could play the piano.

A *wish* is to want something. A *desire* is a longing or craving for something. A wish seldom produces the motivation required to achieve a goal, while real desire almost always produces that motivation. Desire can apply to something that is very pure or very base. It is easy to have natural man desires; that is the "natural" thing to do. But, to do the Lord's will and create righteous desires takes effort and self discipline—

all contrary to the natural state. President David O. McKay quoted the following to make this point:

### Soul That Resists Desire

It is easy enough to be virtuous
When nothing tempts you to stray,
When without or within no voice of sin
Is luring your soul away.
But it is only a negative virtue
Until it is tried by fire,
And the soul that is worth the honor of earth
Is the soul that resists desire.[2]

* Arabian horses are known for their intelligence, loyalty, stamina, and speed. Over the centuries they have been used for battle, raiding, protection, and in the service of royalty. They are often exported and bred with other horses to add refinement, speed, and endurance. One of the ancient training methods used to identify an elite Arabian horse was the whistle test. If a horse could pass this test, it was used for the most important missions. It was the final test of a horse's ability to master its desires.

The horse was corralled over a long period with no water. The test began as the gate was opened and the horse was allowed to see and smell cool water. As soon as the horse ran for the water, the trainer blew his whistle, the signal for the horse to come to him. The horse would do one of these things:

- Pay no attention to the whistle
- Drink and then obey the whistle
- Obey the whistle immediately

The horses chosen for the most important missions were those that obeyed the whistle first, forgetting their need for water.

The same principle that applies to horses also applies to humans; many are called but few are chosen because they are not willing to pay the price. Some let the natural man dominate their lives, making little effort to control those base desires. Others want to straddle the fence, drinking in the things of the world while still trying to obey the call of righteousness. You can either be hot or cold, but you can't be both. Christ described those who try: "I know thy works, that thou art neither cold nor hot: I would thou wert cold or hot" (Revelations 3:15). On the other hand, there are those who are obedient to the spiritual whistle. Jesus called them his sheep: "My sheep hear my voice, and I know them, and they follow me" (John 10:27). Do you answer the whistle?

## RESPOND TO CHALLENGES

People respond to challenges; they don't respond to begging. I have had plenty of opportunity to learn that lesson over the years. While serving in a bishopric, I worked with the teachers quorum. Part of my responsibility was to help young men understand their potential. A ninth grader in the quorum was a runner for his school and had clocked close to a five-minute-mile—an impressive time for his age group. He had major college potential as a scholar and as an athlete, but he seemed to lack the desire to do what was required to earn a scholarship. He was so bright that he never took a book home but still made straight A's in school. Without discipline, his natural abilities would not take him too far in life. Running was a way for this boy to develop that discipline. Hoping to create a stronger desire within him, I decided to challenge him. I told him that if he broke a five-minute mile at his next track meet, I would buy him a steak dinner at the restaurant of his choice. The next Saturday, he ran a 4:42 mile and broke not only his school record but also the school district record for a ninth grader.

If responding to a reward from others motivates you, try challenging and rewarding yourself. I have noticed that by pushing myself in little increments I can create a desire to do more; success breeds success. President Spencer W. Kimball called it "lengthening your stride." He said, "Present levels of performance are not acceptable either to ourselves or to the Lord. In saying that, I am not calling for flashy, temporary differences in our performance levels, but a quiet resolve . . . to do a better job—to lengthen our stride."[3]

My wife and I traveled to Egypt and Israel several years ago. A young man named Mike and his wife of eleven months were with us on that trip. He suffered from multiple sclerosis and could not participate in the more rigorous activities on our tour. His condition prevented him from climbing Mount Sinai in Egypt, even though he had a strong desire to do so. On the starlit night before our group was to climb Mount Sinai, we held a meeting below the mountain. We sang, "I Am a Child of God." The words "lead me, guide me, *walk* beside me" resonated with Mike. He knew how much he needed the Lord to walk beside him in his illness.

Later in Jerusalem, many in our group decided to go through Hezekiah's tunnel. This tunnel was dug in Jerusalem about 701 BC during the reign of King Hezekiah. Designed as an aqueduct to provide Jerusalem with water during an impending siege by the Assyrians, the tunnel is 533 meters long. It is pitch black, requiring a flashlight. At some points you have to bend down because of the low ceiling, and there are times when waist-deep water still flows through the tunnel. My wife and I did not have proper shoes for the walk, and Mike did not plan to go either because of his medical condition. His wife Kim decided to go through with the group, and Mike stayed behind with Wendy and me.

After Kim entered the tunnel, someone handed Mike a pair of water shoes, in case he changed his mind. I could see on his face the memory of all of the times he had had to stay behind. I could also see the desire he had to share this experience with his wife. He got off the bus and walked into the tunnel, without a flashlight. If he didn't catch up with Kim, he would be putting the words of the song to the test: "walk beside me."

Wendy and I worried and waited at the top of the hill near the exit of the tunnel. When Kim appeared without Mike, I asked where he was. She looked terrified when she realized he was alone in the dark tunnel. We all stood anxiously waiting for Mike to exit the tunnel. Soon, people from other groups began coming out who had entered long after Mike. Now Kim was beside herself. Two men in our group offered to go back into the tunnel to find him. They were gone a long time, and everyone in the group began praying for Mike's safety. Finally, he emerged with the two men on either side of him holding him up. We cheered for him as he and his wife embraced.

Mike had a desire to experience the tunnel and his desire drove him to complete that mission. All of us who were watching learned that the Lord will lead us and guide us if we have the desire and determination to act in faith. President Kimball said, "It is in the doing that the real blessing comes. Do it! That's our motto."[4]

In a conversation with Elder Christoffel Golden before he was called as a General Authority, I learned about the faithful people he worked with in his assignment with the Church Educational System in Eastern Africa. He recalled attending an inservice meeting in Zimbabwe where the CES coordinator presented teacher recognition awards. One man singled out for recognition was an early morning seminary teacher who taught twenty students in a rural area. This teacher left home every morning at 3:30 AM. He rode his bicycle to the home of one of his seminary students, stopped, and knocked on the door. That student then ran beside his teacher's bicycle until reaching the next student's home. They continued stopping at students' homes until they gathered all twenty students. They arrived at the building to start seminary at 6 AM. After class, the teacher and his students repeated this process until all were delivered back to their homes.

When the teacher was called forward to receive his award, Elder Golden expected a young man. Instead, he was surprised to see an old man, hunched over with arthritis. Elder Golden talked to the coordinator afterward and asked how the youth responded to this teacher. He replied that the students loved him and that when he was in the front of the class, he was like a flower blooming.

This seminary teacher loved the Lord and had a strong desire to achieve what he was called to do. The desire overcame the difficulty of the task. The Lord makes many promises to those who have desire. He promises that, "If you desire, you shall be the means of doing much good in this generation" (Doctrine and Covenants 6:8).

You may think you do not have the capacity to accomplish anything great or grand, but that is not the case. President Hinckley said, "The work of the world is not done by intellectual geniuses. It is done by men of ordinary capacity who use their abilities in an extraordinary manner."[5] Also, Thomas Edison spoke from experience when he said, "Many of life's failures are men who did not realize how close they were to success when they gave up."[6] If you desire to do your part, your

Heavenly Father will lead you, guide you, and walk beside you until you achieve the goal he sent you to accomplish.

———————

Notes

1. Royden G. Derrick, "The Way to Perfection," *Ensign*, May 1989, 76.
2. David O. McKay, "Worth While" in Conference Report, April 1965, 81.
3. Spencer W. and Edward L. Kimball, *Teachings of Spencer W. Kimball*, 174.
4. Spencer W. Kimball, "Applying the Principles of Welfare Services," *Ensign*, May 1979, 98.
5. Gordon B. Hinckley, "Watch the Switches in Your Life," *Ensign*, January 1973, 91.
6. Thomas Edison, worldofinspiration.com.

# CHAPTER 14

# BE CONSISTENT
# AND PERSEVERE

*That which we persist in doing becomes easier,*
*not that the task itself has become easier, but*
*that our ability to perform it has improved.*

—Ralph Waldo Emerson

Hundreds of runners flock to a sprawling park in my hometown each Thanksgiving Day for a 5K (3.1-mile) "Turkey Trot" consisting of two laps around the park. Since many members of our stake participate each year, our young family decided to attend to cheer them on. Several of the sons of our stake president were participating that year, but we were surprised to see their father lacing up his shoes, too. As far as I knew, he had never before attempted a race. A "Golden Gloves" boxer in his younger years, he had apparently rediscovered his Everlast boxing trunks and was wearing them that morning. Snickers rippled through the crowd, since his attire didn't quite match the couture of the other runners. No one knew he had been training for weeks.

I assumed our stake president was out for a leisurely "fun run" and was surprised when he took off at a fast clip. I wondered if he knew what he was doing. After a while the crowd began to cheer as the college runners passed the halfway point at the first lap. Next in line were the very good high school runners receiving more cheers from the crowd. Soon I heard some of our stake members cheering and looked up to see our stake president still running almost as fast as he had started.

As the crowd cheered he broke into a sprint as if he were nearing the finish line. But just after passing the main crowd, he slowed to a walk and then stopped at the side of the course. Breathing heavily, he looked extremely pleased with himself, as if he had gone the distance.

I approached him with the bad news: "President, you do realize that this race is *two* laps around the park, don't you? You're at the halfway point." I'll never forget the look on his face; he thought he was done. With resolution, he turned and, at a very slow jog, reentered the race. Even children were passing him now. He finished behind the pack with those who had jogged a little and walked a little that day.

Starting off strong does not mean that you will necessarily finish strong. Consistency is much more important than bursts of brilliance interspersed with fading and failure. When I joined a new gym, I disciplined myself to go every weekday. As I walked out the door each day, the guy at the front desk said, "Have a good day!" I always thanked him, and then responded with something similar. He consistently said the same thing every day for months. Then, one day he said something that I took as a great compliment: "I'll see you tomorrow." What a great feeling to have someone recognize that I was consistent.

Your "life" mission is called that for a reason. It is not a two-day mission or a two-month mission. It takes constant, steady effort over a lifetime. Paul, speaking to the Hebrews, referred to such consistency: "Wherefore seeing we also are compassed about with so great a cloud of witnesses, let us lay aside every weight, and the sin which doth so easily beset us, and let us run with patience the race that is set before us" (Hebrews 12:1).

Throughout history we see examples of those who started off their life mission by "racing" quickly and then fizzling in the end. In biblical history, David went from being a common shepherd boy to a national hero when he killed Goliath. He then went from being a great king and spiritual giant with a special mission to a "has been." His immorality with Bathsheba led to the death of her husband, and, as a result, David lost his family and his exaltation (see Doctrine and Covenants 132:39). He started the race running at the head of the pack but ended up being disqualified. David's son Solomon also started off his mission very quickly, even seeing Christ. However, he, too, faded from the race.

Benedict Arnold started off as a strong patriot but finished as a traitor. Judas Iscariot began as a faithful disciple and one of the Lords' chosen apostles. He ended up betraying Christ for thirty pieces of silver and later hanged himself (see Matthew 27:5). Each day the headlines tell the stories of men and women with great potential who don't finish the race.

One of the most talented and capable men of this dispensation was Oliver Cowdery. Joseph Smith's first history states the "Lord appeared unto . . . Oliver Cowdery and shewed unto him the plates in a vision and . . . what the Lord was about to do through me, his unworthy servant. Therefore he was desirous to come and write for me to translate."[1] Oliver described many of the events he was involved in with eloquent words revealing his great talents. Consider the following statements:

**Book of Mormon Scribe:** "These were days never to be forgotten—to sit under the sound of a voice dictated by the inspiration of heaven, awakened the utmost gratitude of this bosom! Day after day I continued, uninterrupted to write from his mouth, as he translated with the Urim and Thummim, or, as the Nephites would have said, 'Interpreters,' the history or record called the Book of Mormon."[2]

**Aaronic Priesthood:** "Then his voice, though mild, pierced to the center, and his words, 'I am thy fellow-servant,' dispelled every fear. We listened, we gazed, we admired! 'Twas the voice of an angel from glory, 'twas a message from the Most High! And as we heard we rejoiced, while His love enkindled upon our souls, and we were wrapped in the vision of the Almighty! Where was room for doubt? Nowhere; uncertainty had fled, doubt had sunk no more to rise, while fiction and deception had fled forever!"[3]

**Kirtland Temple Dedication:** "I saw the glory of God, like a great cloud, come down and rest upon the house. . . . I also saw cloven tongues like as of fire rest upon many . . . while they spake with other tongues and prophesied."[4]

In addition, Oliver was a participant in some of the seminal moments in Church history:

- Recipient of the Melchizedek Priesthood from Peter, James, and John (1829)

- One of Three Witnesses to the Book of Mormon (1829)

- One of the charter members of the Church (1830)

- First scribe to assist Joseph Smith in translating the Bible

- Leader of the first major Church mission to the Lamanites in Missouri (1830)

- Ordination to the High Priesthood (1831)

- Along with John Whitmer, took revelations to Missouri for printing (1831)

- Member of the Kirtland High Council (1834)

- Ordained Assistant President of the Church (1834)

- Assistant in choosing the Twelve Apostles (1835)

- Appointed as Church recorder (1835)

- Recipient with Joseph Smith of priesthood keys from Elijah, Elias, and Moses (1836)

After being involved in so many miraculous events, Oliver was excommunicated for apostasy in 1838. He remained estranged from the Church until 1848, when Orson Hyde rebaptized him.

Oliver had a mission to help lay the foundation of a great latter-day work. He started off the race swiftly but ended up dropping out. By the time he reentered the race it was too late to accomplish part of his mission, and he lost his right to continue. President Joseph Fielding Smith explained what he thought Oliver could have done:

Had Oliver Cowdery remained true, had he been faithful to his testimony and his calling as the 'Second Elder' and Assistant

President of the Church, I am just as satisfied as I am that I am here that Oliver Cowdery would have gone to Carthage with the Prophet Joseph Smith and laid down his life instead of Hyrum Smith. That would have been his right. Maybe it sounds a little strange to speak of martyrdom as being a right, but it was a right. Oliver Cowdery lost it and Hyrum Smith received it. According to the law of witnesses—and this is a divine law—it had to be.[5]

Another early Church member who started his life at a sprint was Lyman Wight. I have a special interest in him since the institute building where I work is just a few miles from where he once lived with his followers. The Lord called him "my servant" seven times in the Doctrine and Covenants. Oliver Cowdery baptized him in 1830. He traveled with Zion's Camp and was later ordained an Apostle by Joseph Smith.

On one occasion Moses Wilson, an enemy of the Church, tried to bribe Lyman to swear testimony against Joseph Smith. Wight replied, "General, you are entirely mistaken in your man, both in regard to myself and Joseph Smith. Joseph Smith is not an enemy to mankind; he is not your enemy, and is as good a friend as you have got. Had it not been for him, you would have been in hell long ago, for I should have sent you there, and no other man than Joseph Smith could have prevented me, and you may thank him for your life. And now, if you will give me the boys I brought from Diahman yesterday, I will whip your whole army."

General Wilson said, "Wight, you are a strange man; but if you will not accept my proposal, you will be shot tomorrow morning at eight."

Wight replied, "Shoot and be damned."[6]

Indicating his strong-willed personality, Lyman was dubbed "The Wild Ram of the Mountains" by William W. Phelps. He was called as leader of the Wisconsin-based Black River Lumber Company, responsible for cutting lumber for the construction of the Nauvoo temple. When Lyman finished that assignment, Joseph Smith called him to take a group of Saints to homestead in Texas.

But, when Joseph was killed in 1844, something died in Lyman as well. "The only man in the world that can control me is now gone," he said.[7] He disassociated himself from Brigham Young and the other Apostles and led his group to Texas against the pleas of his brethren to help finish the Nauvoo temple first. His refusal to unite with the other Apostles finally led to his excommunication in 1848. Lyman died in Texas ten years later. After his death, his little colony broke up and scattered. Of his 150 to 200 followers, there were no known faithful church members who remained in Texas.

Contrast Lyman's story with that of William Williamson, who was born in New Orleans, Louisiana in 1829. His father died when he was about three years old, and his mother died when he was thirteen. He and his brother George ended up working for a Catholic rancher of French descent in Welch, Louisiana. William married the rancher's daughter Joissine in 1854. He fought for the South during the Civil War. After returning home, he moved his family to southeast Texas. There were no Catholic churches in the area, so Joissine attended the Baptist Church, but William refused to join her. He remained aloof from organized religion, although he was a very religious man. By the end of 1899, William was in bad health. As the year turned into a new century, two missionaries happened to come upon the Williamson's home after becoming lost in rain and fog. William listened to their message and, along with his wife, entered the waters of baptism in April 1900. Their youngest daughter Epsie, my grandmother, followed them in August of that year.

William did not become a scribe to a prophet. He was not a member of a high council, nor did he see angels. He was just a common Texas farmer who accepted the truth when he heard it and remained consistent for the rest of his life. That life ended just seven months after his baptism, but his consistency, and that of his wife, was enough. She was a faithful member of the Church and great missionary until her death in 1912. My great grandparents now have more than four thousand descendants, most of them faithful Church members in Texas.

Those men and women who drop out of the race because of tragic mistakes, like Lyman Wight and Oliver Cowdery, are probably not the norm. More typical are those with big plans who lose interest or slow their pace and run out of time. How many missions are sitting on shelves because those assigned to them are not working consistently?

There are legions of starters but few finishers.

You may see the results of inconsistency all around. You start a scripture-reading program and do well for a while but then taper off and stop. You start a diet, join a gym, register for a class, get a library card, and buy a tennis racquet. Then you lose desire and energy.

Those who remain consistent are a rare pleasure to watch. The grandfather of one of our daughters-in-law received an award from his employer at retirement for having perfect attendance at work for forty straight years. Several of my brother's children not only had perfect attendance for four years of early morning seminary, they also had perfect attendance for twelve straight years of school. One of the grandmothers of a personal friend was praised in general conference for completing 20,000 temple endowment sessions during her lifetime.

At the end of one semester when I was teaching at BYU, I was recording final test scores and averaging final grades. Occasionally a test would be placed in the wrong pile, so I didn't think much about it when at first I couldn't find Paul's final exam score. However, after searching everywhere, I began to suspect that I had lost it, or that he had never taken the test. Since he had an A average in the class, I was fairly certain that the problem was mine and not his. Without the final, his semester grade would drop from an A to a D minus. I had to be sure it was not my mistake. I searched the student directory but found no phone number for him. I called the campus operator but there was no listing in his name. After making a series of calls to other class members, I finally got what I hoped was his phone number. When the person at the other end of the phone answered, I asked for Paul.

"This is Paul."

I asked him if he was enrolled in my class, and he said that he was. I was relieved, yet embarrassed to inform him that I must have lost his final, since I had no record that he had taken it.

"No, I never got around to taking it."

I was taken aback by the casual tone of his voice. However, being in the Christmas spirit, I told him that I was going to be in my office for the next six hours. If he would just come and take the test, I would overlook the fact that he hadn't taken it when he was supposed to.

"I'll think about it."

I waited for him to show up and mentally prepared a little lecture about gratitude and taking advantage of opportunities at BYU. Thousands of students who would love to attend the university are turned away every year. My little lecture was never given because he never showed up to take the test. I waited until the last minute when the grades had to be turned in, and had no choice but to give him a D minus. During the holidays, I thought a lot about Paul and how he had blown a whole semester grade because he had not endured to the end. Simply because he did not show up for one day, the twenty-eight days when he was in class counted for nothing in terms of his grade.

Heavenly Father makes it possible for you to come to earth and take a series of classes. Some students will do very well for a while and then just give up for whatever reason. Ralph Waldo Emerson once said, "That which we persist in doing becomes easier, not that the task itself has become easier, but that our ability to perform it has improved."[8] Being consistent simply makes life easier. It is not enough to keep the commandments for a time. It is not enough to realize that you have a mission and then make a tentative stab at it, or to stop before the finish line.

Giving up at the end can lose a lifetime of effort. President Heber J. Grant counseled, "All who are laboring in the improvement cause should be true to themselves, and when they resolve to accomplish something, they should labor cheerfully and with a determination until the promise to themselves has become a reality."[9] You were not sent to earth to start with a blaze of glory and then put up your feet.

President Hinckley told a story of looking at the night sky with his brother. He was fascinated with the North Star because it was consistent. No matter what the earth's rotation was, the North Star never moved. He said, "I recognized it as a constant in the midst of change. It was something that could always be counted on, something that was dependable, an anchor in what otherwise appeared to be a moving and unstable firmament."[10] In many ways President Hinckley became like the North Star. He did not burn out nor even dim; in fact he picked up the pace as he grew older. Let his example be the star to follow in your quest for consistency.

## Notes

1. Daniel H. Ludlow, ed., *Encyclopedia of Mormonism*, 335.
2. Oliver Cowdery, *Times and Seasons*, vol. 2, no. 1, November 1, 1840, 201.
3. Joseph Smith, *History of the Church*, 1:43.
4. Ludlow, *Encyclopedia of Mormonism*, 426.
5. Joseph Fielding Smith, *Doctrines of Salvation*, vol. 1, 221.
6. Hyrum M. Smith and Janne M. Sjodahl, *Doctrine and Covenants Commentary, Containing Revelations Given to Joseph Smith*, 311.
7. Henry D. Taylor, "A Time of Testing," *Ensign*, December 1971, 43.
8. Ralph Waldo Emerson, wiki.wsmoak.net.
9. Heber J. Grant, "The Nobility of Labor," *Ensign*, March 1972, 68.
10. Sheri L. Dew, *Go Forward with Faith: The Biography of Gordon B. Hinckley*, 5–6.

# CHAPTER 15

# ELIMINATE PROCRASTINATION

*Procrastination . . . is the thief of eternal life.*

—Joseph Fielding Smith

There are two entries in my personal journal, fifteen years apart, that I share here with some embarrassment, in hopes you will learn from my mistakes:

> **January 21, 1982:** Last Monday, Wendy and I finished listening to a cassette tape called *Eliminating Self-defeating Behaviors*, by Jonathan Chamberlain. I also purchased a book on the subject. The idea is to choose a behavior to work on that you feel is holding you back in your progression . . . I chose procrastination as the self-defeating behavior that I would most like to eliminate in my life. As part of the program, I had to write when and how I did this behavior. It was hard to admit how often I procrastinated and the clever rationalizations I came up with to justify my behavior . . . But the real eye-opener was to count the cost of hanging onto the behavior. It was a real revelation to me to see how much a self-defeating behavior can stop the progress of your life. Since finishing the tape and book, I have become very aware of the problem and have a desire to eliminate it from my life. I feel good that I have accomplished a great deal since beginning the program this week.

Several subsequent journal entries told of the great progress I was making in overcoming my problem with procrastination. Over the course of the next few weeks, the entries regarding this subject trailed off and eventually stopped. Then fifteen years later came this entry:

> **October 27, 1997:** Lately I have been reading a book called *Eliminating Self-Defeating Behaviors* by Jonathan Chamberlain. It has been sitting in my bookcase untouched for years. I remember working on some self-defeating behaviors long ago, but I can't remember what they were. Something told me that I should go through the process again and try to eliminate a behavior that seems to be holding me back. The biggest problem I have right now in my life is that I am a huge procrastinator. I put off everything you can think of. I was very aware today of my problem and how much it is holding me back. I don't procrastinate nearly as much at work as I do at home. I should be getting much more done at home and during my free time than what I do . . . I am going to face this problem again, but it will not be easy, and I know it. I have hung onto it for so long that it is going to be very hard to overcome. I did get a lot done today, however, and I hope tomorrow to face my problem even more. If I could just stay aware, I believe I could lessen the behavior in my life.

Comparing those entries many years after the fact made me think back to an old saying I heard while working in sales for 3M Business Products. My supervisor said something about human behavior and I thought he was making a joke. Now I believe him. He said that *a person twenty-one years old or older will continue to do in the future as they have done in the past, unless they have a spiritual experience or brain surgery.*

I learned a valuable lesson looking back on these two entries. Procrastination is a quality of the natural man and does not simply go away by itself. It takes constant awareness and effort to overcome this handicap. We have been warned against it many times: "And now, as I said unto you before, as ye have had so many witnesses, therefore, I beseech of you that ye do not procrastinate the day of your repentance until the end; for after this day of life, which is given us to prepare for eternity, behold, if we do not improve our time while in this life, then cometh the night of darkness wherein there can be no labor performed" (Alma 34:33).

Many of us rationalize our procrastination as if it were inconsequential. We tell ourselves that we are really busy and need to slow down. It temporarily soothes us to say that we will get around to something tomorrow. As the old saying goes, "Procrastination is a silly thing, it only makes me sorrow; but I can change at any time—I think I will tomorrow!"[1]

The majority of folks I associate with every day are college students. I get many of my life lessons from them. Most are remarkable examples of people with high goals who are working hard to achieve those goals. A few struggle to achieve what they set out to do. The college years are unique in that students have more freedom than in any other phase of their adult lives. Most students are only required to attend class for twelve to sixteen hours a week. In contrast, elementary, middle, and high school students are normally required to be in school about thirty-five hours per week. There are no truant officers in college to enforce attendance, and many professors do not take roll. College students are expected to spend the majority of their time studying outside of class. However, there is no one to check whether this is done.

Students with light class loads do not tend to make better grades than those with far more rigorous schedules. For some reason, procrastination seems to be a bigger temptation for students with light loads than for those with more demanding schedules. More time does not always equal higher productivity. If you want something done, get a busy person to do it.

Observing college students causes me to examine myself and ask how I waste time. I have heard students complain loudly about how "busy" they are, even though they have been hanging out at the institute for hours. They moan about how tired they are after pulling an all-nighter, finishing assignments they have put off until the last minute. Such rationalizing comes easily to the natural man. He is so self-satisfied with his busyness attending to the day's tasks that he never gets around to the important things.

A story is told about a little boy who came home from school one day and had one C and five F's on his report card. His father demanded an explanation. The boy said, "I guess I just spent too much time in one subject." If you are going to achieve what you were sent to achieve, you will need to pick up the pace and spend time in every subject related to that mission. While some treat procrastination as a joke, as seen through God's eyes, it is no laughing matter.

## CONSEQUENCES OF PROCRASTINATION

To overcome a human weakness, it helps to count the cost of the defect. For example, cigarettes should be far less of a temptation when the smoker realizes they cause lung cancer and many other diseases. Although there is no Surgeon General's warning stamped on procrastination, it can be spiritually deadly.

**Procrastination is addictive:** President Spencer W. Kimball said, "One of the most serious human defects in all ages is procrastination, an unwillingness to accept personal responsibilities now. Men came to earth consciously to obtain their schooling, their training and development, and to perfect themselves, but many have allowed themselves to be diverted and have become merely 'hewers of wood and drawers of water,' addicts to mental and spiritual indolence and to the pursuit of worldly pleasure."[2]

**Procrastination leads to emptiness, lack of fulfillment, and unhappiness:** Elder William H. Bennett said, "Procrastination, which is the practice of putting off, intentionally and habitually, those things that should be done in a timely manner, not only wastes time; but it leaves our lives empty, unfulfilled, and unhappy."[3]

**Procrastination kills progress:** Elder Marvin J. Ashton said, "We are living in a time of urgency. We are living in a time of spiritual crisis. We are living in a time close to midnight. There is an urgency to meet the worldwide spiritual crisis through action now. It can only be accomplished by performance. Procrastination is a deadly weapon of human progress."[4]

**Procrastination blocks peace of mind:** Elder Joseph B. Wirthlin said, "One habit that prevents inner peace is procrastination. It clutters our minds with unfinished business and makes us uneasy until we finish a task and get it out of the way."[5]

**Procrastination steals happiness:** Elder Henry B. Eyring said, "And so Satan tempts with procrastination throughout our days of probation. Any choice to delay repentance gives him the chance to steal happiness from one of the spirit children of our Heavenly Father."[6]

**Procrastination leads to malaise:** Marvin J. Ashton said, "How comfortable some of us become as we nestle in the web of procrastination. It is a false haven of rest for those who are content to live without purpose, commitment, or self-discipline."[7]

**Procrastination is a thief:** President Kimball said, "Procrastination—thou wretched thief of time and opportunity!"[8] Elder Reed Smoot said, "There is nothing that steals man's time, his talents, his vigor, his energy, even his prospects of salvation, in greater degree than the crime of procrastination."[9] President Thomas S. Monson said, "It is the thief of our self-respect. It nags at us and spoils our fun. It deprives us of the fullest realization of our ambitions and hopes."[10] President Joseph Fielding Smith said, "Procrastination . . . is the thief of eternal life."[11]

Clearly procrastination ranks as one of the most debilitating of all human deficiencies, eating away at our progress in small, almost imperceptible increments. An old saying states, "There is less chance of losing eternal life by a blowout than by a series of slow leaks!"

## WHAT IS YOUR DISTRACTION?

When you procrastinate doing the things you should, it is usually because you are spending your time doing something less important. To eliminate procrastination, closely examine how you spend your time.

A few years ago a young man I will call Mike came to see me. He was a very depressed twenty-eight-year-old returned missionary, who was still living with his parents. He was working at menial, low paying jobs and had never sought an education past high school. When I asked him to describe how he felt, he said, "Well, I don't plan to run out in front of a truck, but I would not be upset if I got killed going home." Then he admitted that he had contemplated suicide. He said he was plagued with insomnia and that he tossed and turned all night long. Mike was searching for answers and wanted my help.

I asked him why he had never gone to college; he had no answer. I asked him if he had ever taken a college entrance exam, and he said he had. I was shocked when he revealed his scores. He easily could have been admitted into most universities in America. As he talked, my watch caught the sunlight that reflected right onto the face of Jesus Christ, whose picture was hanging in my office. That was my que.

"What is at the center of your life?" I asked. He didn't know. "What do you think your life mission is; what were you sent here to do?" He didn't know. I finally asked him if I could get really personal with him.

"When was the most happy and spiritual time of your life?"

"My mission."

"Why then?"

"Because I was totally focused on missionary work."

"Why aren't you focused on it now if it brought you so much happiness?"

"I don't know."

"What time did you get up while on your mission?"

"6 AM."

"What else did you do on your mission?"

"I read the scriptures, prayed, fasted, helped others, wrote in my journal, exercised, limited my eating, and attended church a lot."

I kept asking questions, hoping he would see what he was doing to himself. I told him the next set of questions only applied to the last ninety days of his life and that he would have to estimate some of the answers: "How many days did you . . .

| | |
|---|---|
| Get up at 6 AM? | "12 of 90" |
| Limit your food intake? | "5 of 90" |
| Exercise? | "0 of 90" |
| Fast? | "1 of 90" |
| Make home teaching visits? | "5 of 15 expected visits" |
| Write in your journal? | "0 of 90" |
| Have morning prayers? | "15 of 90" |
| Have evening prayers? | "30 of 90" |
| Attend church? | "10 of 12 Sundays" |

Mike had now revealed that he was not doing any of the things associated with happiness on his mission, except going to church. It was time to see how he *was* spending his time, and I knew that he was about to get even more uncomfortable. But he had asked for help so I pressed forward. I led him through a normal day to see how much time he spent in various pursuits.

First, he told me how much time he spent watching TV, but admitted his estimate might have been low. I already guessed that because he knew far too much about far too many programs. He wasn't sure how much time he devoted to listening to music every day, but acknowledged that the radio was frequently on in his truck and in his room. I asked him what time he turned his music on in the morning and what time he turned it off at night. "I never turn it off," he said. No wonder he had insomnia. He had complained that he didn't feel like his prayers were being answered but admitted the radio was on during prayer time too.

After more probing questions, we were able to put together a rough estimate of where his time had been spent during the prior ninety days, outside of church and work:

| | |
|---|---|
| Praying: | 130 minutes |
| Reading Scriptures: | 630 minutes |
| Writing in Journal: | 0 minutes |
| Exercising: | 0 minutes |
| **Total Time** | about 11 hours in 90 days |
| | |
| TV/Movies | 10,800 minutes |
| Radio/Music | 64,800 minutes |
| **Total time** | about 1,260 hours in 90 days |

Here was a depressed returned missionary who was spending over 100 times more with the media than he was with the things that had brought him happiness on his mission. Mike was visibly stunned and humbled when he looked at where his time was going. I was straightforward with him and told him it was time to commit to doing the things that had made him happy on his mission. He enrolled in college that year and began to experience a mighty change. He married in the temple and now has several children.

Examine where your time goes and eliminate the things that promote procrastination. President Kimball once said, "In my office at home in Salt Lake City, I have a little sign and it says, 'Do it!' I suppose if I have learned anything in life, it is that we are to keep moving, keep trying—as long as we breathe! If we do, we will be surprised at how much more can still be done."[12] I went home from that first visit with Mike asking myself a question that you should consider. Does the way I spend my time harmonize with my mission in life?

# CHOOSE TODAY

Elder Neal A. Maxwell taught, "Joshua didn't say choose you next year whom you will serve; he spoke of 'this day,' while there is still daylight and before the darkness becomes more and more normal." (See Joshua 24:15.)[13]

When Jesus Christ was on earth he chose twelve apostles. When he called Simon and Andrew, "He saith unto them, Follow me, and I will make you fishers of men. And they *straightway* left their nets, and followed him" (Matthew 4:19–20). There was no hesitation from those two brethren. What a powerful example of not letting procrastination delay your mission.

Paul exemplified in his conversion a perfect response to his calling: "And Ananias went his way, and entered into the house; and putting his hands on him said, Brother Saul, the Lord, [even] Jesus, that appeared unto thee in the way as thou camest, hath sent me, that thou mightest receive thy sight, and be filled with the Holy Ghost. And immediately there fell from his eyes as it had been scales: and he received sight forthwith, and arose, and was baptized. And when he had received meat, he was strengthened. Then was Saul certain days with the disciples which were at Damascus. And *straightway* he preached Christ in the synagogues, that he is the Son of God" (Acts 9:17–20, emphasis added).

Elder Marvin J. Ashton called *straightway* a "power word," and an "action word." "It means immediately, without delay or hesitation. It means at once. Also, it is associated with having no curve or turn—a straight course, track, or path. Procrastination would be the very opposite of straightway. To procrastinate is to put off intentionally and habitually something that should be done. Procrastination is unproductive delay."[14]

Much needs to be accomplished in the short and uncertain time you have in mortality. President Thomas S. Monson declared: "How fragile life, how certain death. We do not know when we will be required to leave this mortal existence. And so I ask, 'What are we doing with today?' If we live only for tomorrow, we'll eventually have a lot of empty yesterdays. Have we been guilty of declaring, 'I've been thinking about making some course corrections in my life. I plan to take the first step—tomorrow?' With such thinking, tomorrow is forever. Such tomorrows rarely come unless we do something about them today. As the familiar hymn teaches:

> There are chances for work all around just now,
> Opportunities right in our way.
> Do not let them pass by, saying, 'Sometime I'll try,'
> But go and do something today."[15]

It is time that you straightway go and do what you have been assigned to do. It is time to eliminate procrastination from your life.

---

Notes

1.  Marvin J. Ashton, "Straightway," *Ensign*, May 1983, 30.
2.  Spencer W. and Edward L. Kimball, *Teachings of Spencer W. Kimball*, 48.
3.  William J. Bennett, "Inertia," *Ensign*, May 1974, 33.
4.  Marvin J. Ashton, "A Time of Urgency," *Ensign*, May 1974, 35.
5.  Joseph B. Wirthlin, "Peace Within," *Ensign*, May 1991, 36.
6.  Henry B. Eyring, "Do Not Delay," *Ensign*, November 1999, 33.
7.  Ashton, "Straightway," 30.
8.  Kimball, *Teachings of Spencer W. Kimball*, 83.
9.  Reed Smoot, in Conference Report, October 1907, 57–58.
10. Thomas S. Monson, "Learning the ABCs at BYU," *BYU Speeches of the Year*, February 8, 1966, 3.
11. Joseph Fielding Smith, "The Thief of Eternal Life," in Conference Report, April 1969, 121.

12. Kimball, *Teachings of Spencer W. Kimball*, 173.

13. Neal A. Maxwell, "Why Not Now?" *Ensign*, November 1974, 12.

14. Ashton, "Straightway," 30.

15. Thomas S. Monson, "May We So Live," *Ensign*, August 2008, 4–9.

# CHAPTER 16

# MAKE GOOD
# DECISIONS

*You must study it out in your mind;*
*then you must ask me if it be right.*
—Doctrine and Covenants 9:8

When I was a boy, the Church built a new chapel in my hometown, just down the street from my house. It was in the day when members helped in the building process, so I would often walk over to do service and to watch the construction progress. One day several of my friends and I went to the construction site to "help." One of the projects for that day was to pour the cement for the base of the new steeple. After the cement workers left, only my friends and I and the *wet cement* remained behind. Of course a lively discussion ensued. "What could it hurt since it's going to be covered by the steeple anyway? One day we can tell our kids that our names are underneath the steeple at the Church."

Shortly, the names of Marshall Hayes, Randal Wright, Glen Mahana, and others were carefully preserved in the cement. I also put the year under my name—1963. We were quite proud of our work. Several days later the workers came back and finished erecting the steeple. It was exciting to look down the road and see the towering steeple and to know that as long as it stood our names would lie hidden underneath. But when I walked to the church later that day to get a closer view of the new steeple, I was shocked. The base of the steeple was shaped differently from what we had imagined. We had assumed the steeple would cover the concrete foundation, but we were wrong. All four corners were left uncovered. Now, with the steeple completely finished, the name of Marshall Hayes was clearly visible on the left side right next to the main sidewalk going into the chapel and on the right side was "Randal Wright 1963." All of the other names were covered up, but ours were there—a monument to youthful indiscretion.

We got plenty of comments on our impulsive decision from both adults and the other youth of the ward, but there was no going back. And as we quickly found out, sand paper and wire brushes are powerless to erase letters deeply etched in concrete. Finally the entire building was finished and it was time for the dedication. A new Apostle was sent to Southeast Texas on one of his first assignments. We were all expecting an old man. Everyone was surprised to learn that the new Apostle, Thomas S. Monson, was only thirty-six years old. I'm not sure if he looked down and to his right as he inspected the steeple before walking into the chapel that day, but I certainly hope not. And I hope Marshall and I will always stay dedicated to the Lord since our names were part of the building dedicated that day.

Years passed, and we grew up, married, and moved away to attend college. I had no idea at the time I immortalized my name in concrete that one day I would be the institute director at a university near the chapel, and that I would attend church in that building again with my family. I'm sure Marshall didn't realize that day in 1963 that at a future time he would become a prominent orthopedic surgeon in the area and be called President Hayes as he served as a stake president in an area near where that building is located. And every time he goes to visit his parents, he is right next door to the chapel, where his name is still prominently displayed in the steeple base.

One day our oldest son, who was about nine, came home from Cub Scouts and said, "Hey dad, your name is in the steeple at the Church."

"Really?" I quickly tried to change the subject, but it did not work. My mind went back to the day we decided to write our names in the cement and how cool we thought it would be in the future. Now that I was a father, it wasn't nearly as cool as I had expected.

"How did it get there, Dad?"

"Well son, sometimes youth are just so outstanding that the bishop wants to do something in their honor." When he appeared to believe my joke, I decided that I had to come clean and explain how we had made a decision without thinking.

The steeple base has been exposed to the elements for more than four decades, and yet one can still plainly see our names. I am reminded of that choice we made long ago every time I visit my mother and brother, who still attend church in that building. What may seem like small decisions, made on impulse, can linger with us for years or perhaps for a lifetime.

Decisions can change the course of a life either in a positive or negative way. It is through the decision-making process that you achieve your life mission, or fail to attain it. President Henry D. Moyle made this thought-provoking statement: "When in the course of life one arrives at a fork in the way, a decision must be made and a course selected [which] often results in a choice that later becomes completely irrevocable. . . . Our decisions, once executed, can never be erased. This is because such selections introduce a new series of conditions, setting in motion events that cannot later be recalled. The good done, the evil accomplished, are all there."[1]

The newspaper is filled daily with stories of people who make terrible decisions that affect them, and in some cases, countless others for the rest of their lives. Consider the following experience that my wife and I had while shopping at a local grocery store one evening. As I pushed a cart down the aisle, one of the store employees ran by us screaming that there was a man with a gun at the front of the store. He urged us to move toward the back of the store. I thought it was a prank and I continued down the aisle. Soon more employees ran by, yelling for us to head for safety at the back of the store. Wendy followed the others, but my curiosity got the best of me, and I continued to walk up the aisle to see what was going on.

When I got to the end of an aisle, I peeked around the shelves. In the courtesy booth at the front of the store was a young man next to the safe. He had one of the store's female employees by the hair and was holding a gun to her head. She was stuffing cash from the safe into a large brown grocery bag. A sick feeling came over me as I recognized that the young woman being held at gunpoint was Teri, a member of our ward. I wanted to help her but couldn't think of anything to do. I watched helplessly as the gunman yanked her by the hair and screamed orders at her. She was crying and begging him to let her go.

When the bag was filled with money, the robber began moving toward the front doors with Teri as his hostage. As the automatic doors opened, I saw several policemen outside with their guns drawn. A store employee had called 911. I heard a policeman yell, "Let the girl go, let the girl go, put down your gun, put down your gun!" The robber hesitated briefly in the open doorway and then moved out of my line of sight, pulling Teri with him. The automatic doors closed again, and there was a brief silence. Then several gunshots rang out. A sick feeling come over me, but then the front doors opened again and Teri came running back in crying hysterically. Relief washed over me to see she was safe. Apparently when the robber had reached his car, he had pushed her away and told her to run. As soon as she was out of harm's way, the policemen opened fire and seriously wounded the young man.

The next day we found out that the young robber lived a short distance from us and rented a home from some Latter-day Saint friends. He was married with a small child and by all accounts had led a decent life. What led him to rob the supermarket? Apparently he was concerned that he was not providing for his wife and child and he needed money. He then made a terrible mistake by not thinking things through. His decision dramatically changed the course of his life. Once that decision was executed, there was no going back.

Life missions can be altered in minutes by making wrong decisions. No wonder President Ezra Taft Benson said, "Making decisions is probably the most important thing people ever do."[2] We all make thousands of decisions in our lifetime. Some are good decisions and some not so good. How many times have you heard the phrase, "What were you thinking?" That statement usually indicates that you *weren't* thinking. Looking around there is plenty of evidence to back up Henry Ford's statement: "Thinking is the hardest work there is, which is probably the reason so few engage in it."[3]

An old story is told about two friends who took a trip to Canada to go moose hunting. They hired a pilot to fly them into a remote area that was known for trophy moose. They were excited when they got out of the small plane and told the pilot to pick them up in the same location in two days. The hunters each bagged a large moose and waited to be picked up. When the pilot returned, he looked at the size of the two animals and told the hunters that there was no way his plane could get off the ground with that much weight. The hunters both protested and one said, "We came to this exact spot last year, and we both killed the same size moose as these. The pilot last year had a plane just like yours with the same exact engine and he was okay with it." Finally, they convinced the pilot that everything would be fine, and the plane started down the open field. As the pilot tried to gain altitude, he found they were carrying too much weight to clear the tree line, and they crashed. When everyone came to, the dazed hunters looked at each other, and one said, "Where am I?"

His friend looked around and said, "I don't know, but I think we're about thirty-five yards from where we crashed last year!"

This story is played out daily in real headlines about real people who make similarly foolish decisions. Inexplicably, people make the same mistakes they have seen others make, and they repeat their own mistakes with the same tragic outcomes.

## THINKERS

On a trip to Washington D.C., my wife and I visited many of the historical sites, including the monuments to America's founding fathers. They were men sent by God with very specific missions to fulfill. The Lord himself says they were "wise men whom I raised up unto this very purpose" (Doctrine and Covenants 101:80). Their missions were central to the progress of humankind. They were sent to earth to establish a new nation and to write a constitution. In the free nation they helped form, the gospel would be restored and allowed to flourish, and from that great land it would spread to the world. It was no coincidence that George Washington, John Adams, James Madison, Benjamin Franklin, and Thomas Jefferson all lived on earth at the same time and in the same land.

Jefferson was only thirty-three years old when he penned the Declaration of Independence. President John F. Kennedy said at a dinner honoring Nobel laureates: "I think this is the most extraordinary collection of talent, of human knowledge, that has ever been gathered together in the White House—with the possible exception of when Thomas Jefferson dined alone." [4]

How is it possible that America, with a population of 2,327,450 in 1776, produced so many great men at the same time? Their penetrating thinking and decision-making skills have inspired not only their nation, but also people and governments worldwide. It was the same with Joseph Smith and Brigham Young and others whose inspired decisions have blessed millions of lives. Although your mission is quite different from Thomas Jefferson's or Joseph Smith's, you can learn to think more deeply and make better decisions than you sometimes do. Your decisions will affect not only you, but also those who follow after you.

## A DIFFERENT TIME

You live in a time that is very different from your forefathers. Your generation is not known for thinking deeply, nor have you been exposed to many good examples of decision-making skills in a media-saturated society. "Experts" tell you what you should think about every social, mental, legal, and political problem you face. If the president of the United States speaks to the nation, you don't have time to consider what he said before "experts" tell you what it all means. TV celebrities are your role models for courting and marriage. Slick advertising sells you everything you need to be happy, with no money down and no payments due for one year. The last thing some of these purveyors of "happiness" want is for you to think too deeply. But you need to take time to ponder and think about important things in life. Learn to think for yourself and determine where you fit in the plan so you can make good decisions that will lead you in the right paths.

Some decisions in life are critical. For example, who you marry and where you choose to marry that person are subjects the prophets have repeatedly spoken about. This is a decision that will have eternal implications. "Ponder the path of thy feet" (Proverbs 4:26).

The occupation you choose will affect your daily life and play an important part in your ability to carry out the mission you were sent to do. The career you choose may be closely related to your life mission, or at least provide you with the opportunities and resources you need to accomplish it. Many students go through college having no idea what graduation will bring or what they want to do. The following four questions may help those trying to choose a career path:

- Do I have a passion for this field?
- Do I have the skills and talents needed for this field of study?
- Are there job opportunities in this field upon graduation?
- Do I feel right about this major after studying it out carefully and praying for confirmation? (See Doctrine and Covenants 9:8.)

If you cannot say yes to all of these questions, you may be on the wrong career path, or already spinning your wheels in the wrong profession. You may be passionate about Siberian poetry, but a better choice might be to choose a path that will allow you to pay the bills and buy some Siberian poetry books to read after work.

The Lord wants you to think deeply about all the things that will affect your life in a positive or negative way. Someone once said that a used mind is one of the few items that has more value than an unused one. Count the costs and consider the rewards of your decisions.

## How to Make Decisions

In the Doctrine and Covenants, the Lord gave the simplest, yet most powerful counsel ever given for making wise decisions. This clear-cut formula will lead those who follow it to happiness, now and in the future. Decisions based on impulse will be eliminated, and you will be able to do what the Lord expects you to do. The formula was given by the Lord through revelation to the Prophet Joseph Smith: "But, behold, I say unto you, that *you must study it out in your mind*; then *you must ask me if it be right*, and if it is right I will cause that your bosom shall burn within you; therefore, you shall feel that it is right. But if it be not right you shall have no such feelings, but you shall have a stupor of thought that shall cause you to forget the thing which is wrong" (Doctrine and Covenants 9:8–9, emphasis added).

I am convinced that this simple two-step formula would eliminate much of the sorrow and heartbreak in this world and help us achieve our missions in life. Look closely at the Lord's two-part formula.

# PART 1: STUDY IT OUT

The first thing to do with your question is to study it out, which suggests more than a cursory thought. Studying it out means that you consider your decisions from several viewpoints and then ponder what you discover in that process.

# LEARN WHAT THE PROPHETS HAVE SAID

One of the best ways to study things out is to see if the scriptures or the modern prophets have spoken on the subject. For example, we will all face situations on a daily basis where decisions must be made. What movies are okay to see? How do we handle challenges with our children? Your number one rule in making decisions should be to find out what the prophets have already taught on the subject. If you make one decision in life to always obey the prophet's counsel, then you already know what decisions to make in many situations.

I like to keep handy a page of prophetic teachings on any number of subjects that I might face. Then when decision time comes, I can pull out their counsel and make the correct decision. Perhaps your fifteen-year-old daughter will be invited to attend the movies by a seventeen-year-old boy in the ward. She will say it is not a date because "he is just a good friend." By the way, the movie is R-rated, but "all of the other kids in the ward have seen it." It's decision time. What do you do? Go to the prophets' teachings.

> **President Ezra Taft Benson:** "We counsel you . . . not to pollute your minds with such degrading matter, for the mind through which this filth passes is never the same afterwards. Don't see R-rated movies or vulgar videos or participate in any entertainment that is immoral, suggestive, or pornographic."[5]

> **The First Presidency:** "Do not date until you are at least 16 years old. Dating before then can lead to immorality, limit

the number of other young people you meet, and deprive you of experiences that will help you choose an eternal partner."[6]

The prophets have given guidelines on every critical decision you will face in life and many of the not-so-critical ones too. In your study phase, remember that the Lord has said, "Whether by mine own voice or by the voice of my servants, it is the same" (Doctrine and Covenants 1:38).

## THINK OF THE POSSIBLE CONSEQUENCES

A favorite story from the life of President Hinckley takes place early in his mission to England. He was discouraged and wrote a letter to his father, saying: "I am wasting my time and your money. I don't see any point in my staying here." In due time he received a reply from his father: "Dear Gordon. I have your letter . . . I have only one suggestion. Forget yourself and go to work. With love, Your Father."

President Hinckley said of that moment, "I pondered his response and then the next morning in our scripture class we read that great statement of the Lord: 'For whosoever will save his life shall lose it; but whosoever shall lose his life for my sake and the gospel's, the same shall save it'" (Mark 8:35). He then makes this critical point: "That simple statement, that promise, touched me. I got on my knees and made a covenant with the Lord that I would try to forget myself and go to work. I count that as the *day of decision* in my life. Everything good that has happened to me since then I can trace back to the decision I made at that time."[7]

President Hinckley made a decision that changed the course of history. His father's counsel caused him to think deeply. He studied it out, carefully examined himself, and considered the consequences. He then got on his knees and made a covenant with the Lord. He learned lessons on his mission that changed him and in many ways changed the world. What would have been the consequences had he made the decision to come home early instead of completing his mission? How many of your decisions will have important, unforeseen consequences either for good or bad?

# LOOK AT THE FRUITS

Some foolish people feel they need to experiment with all possible choices before making a decision. That may work in an ice cream parlor, but it is a dangerous way to approach life. You don't have to smoke or drink to know that you should not choose that path. All you have to do is look closely to those who have already chosen the path and what the results were. Christ said, "Wherefore by their fruits ye shall know them" (Matt 7:20).

If you see an advertisement for a bar that features "happy hour" every night from 5 PM to 7 PM, you don't have to patronize the bar to determine if it will make you happy. By observing others who center their social lives around the bar scene, you determine if they are genuinely happy. If they are not, then the ad is a lie.

Several years ago, I attended a missionary farewell for an outstanding young man. As part of the service his father spoke. I had known this father for several years and was pleased to see the tremendous progress he had made. Even though he had made some wrong choices in his earlier years, which led to one broken marriage and inactivity in the Church, he had turned his life around. He had been sealed to his second wife and was committed to his Church calling. In his talk he said, "I want everyone here to know that I have been down the wrong path in life." Most in the audience were aware of that. I hoped he was not launching into a confessional at his son's missionary farewell. He continued, "Some of you may be wondering what is down the wrong path and would like to see for yourself what is there. Well, I'll save you the trip, because I've been there, and I can tell you there ain't *nothin'* there!"

There is nothing good at the end of the wrong path in life. The only path to happiness is the straight and narrow path that leads back to God. There is no need to try the scented poisons of Satan when testimonies abound of the misery of people who have succumbed. Look around at those who have chosen to live an immoral lifestyle. What are the consequences of bitter divorces? How many happy drug addicts do you see? Do you know anyone who is pleased with his mound of debts? Is the high school dropout making a good living? Does the unfaithful husband enjoy the respect of his children? Is the unwed teenage mother having fun yet? By constantly looking at the fruits of others' decisions, you can avoid the pitfalls and learn to make wise choices the first time around.

# Pre-Made Decisions

You don't have to wait until you are placed in a tempting situation to go through the Lord's decision-making formula. You can predetermine many of your decisions by studying things out in your mind before being placed in a situation. Dozens of times every day you will come to a fork in the road, beginning with the decision to respond to the alarm, and ending with the choice of bedtime. The time to decide to obey the Word of Wisdom or to remain pure, or to gossip about a friend is long before you are presented with the opportunity. President Kimball counseled, "Make certain decisions only once. We can make a single decision about certain things that we will incorporate in our lives and then make them ours—without having to brood and re-decide a hundred times what it is we will do and what we will not do."[8]

# Part 2: Ask If It Is Right

The second part of the process is much shorter than the first and easy to remember. If you thoroughly study things out in your mind, you can dramatically increase your chances of making a good choice. Sometimes, however, mistakes can still be made, even after pondering. Part two allows the Lord's decision-making process to be foolproof. Involve the Lord in a decision, large or small, by asking if it is right, and then be willing to live with the answer you receive.

"Heavenly Father, I'm trying to decide whether to go into huge debt for a luxury car that I really like and want. Do you think it is the right thing for me to do?"

How do you think he would respond—the one who is all wise and who has your best interests at heart? You have the privilege of asking the very person who sent you to earth with a special mission if a decision you are about to make will help you achieve that mission.

What if every person used this "ask-if-it-be-right" process in making decisions? What would the Spirit whisper to you if you prayed to know if the following actions were the right thing to do?

- Underestimate your taxes
- Break the law of chastity
- Neglect home or visiting teaching
- Drink alcohol
- Wear immodest clothing
- Attend R-rated movies
- Shop on the Sabbath
- Skip church
- View pornography
- Forego paying tithing
- Criticize Church leaders

If you will use the Lord's formula in Doctrine and Covenants 9:8, he will be your partner in decision making, whispering or even shouting the right choice in your mind and in your heart.

---

Notes

1. Henry D. Moyle, in Conference Report, April 1959, 98.
2. Ezra Taft Benson, *Teachings of Ezra Taft Benson*, 386.
3. Henry Ford, *quoteworld.org*
4. William C. Spragens, *Popular Images of American Presidents*, 27.
5. Ezra Taft Benson, "To the Youth of the Noble Birthright," *Ensign*, May 1986, 43.
6. *For the Strength of Youth*, 2001, 24.
7. Jeffrey R. Holland, "President Gordon B. Hinckley: Stalwart and Brave He Stands," *Ensign*, June 1995, 8.
8. Spencer W. Kimball, "Set Some Personal Goals," *Ensign*, May 1976, 46.

# CHAPTER 17

# KEEP PHYSICALLY FIT

*We will regard our body as a temple of our very own. We
will not let it be desecrated or defaced in any way. We
will control our diet and exercise for physical fitness.*

—Russell M. Nelson

W hen I was nineteen years old, I received a large envelope in the
mail from the president informing me of the call I had been
expecting for weeks. It should have been a very exciting day for my
family and me, but instead it produced a sick feeling in the pit of my
stomach. Instead of a welcome mission call from President David O.
McKay, it was a draft notice from U.S. President Lyndon B. Johnson.
The Tet Offensive of the Vietnam War was raging. More than 80,000
North Vietnamese soldiers and the Vietcong, their communist allies in
South Vietnam, had launched relentless attacks on hundreds of South
Vietnamese cities. It was the largest offensive to date against South
Vietnam and its American allies. President Johnson's solution was a
build-up of American troops, and my name was on the list of draft-age
young men.

The demands of the draft had already prompted the Church to
strike a deal with the draft agency, the Selective Service Commission,
to limit the number of missionaries to one per ward every six months,
and my ward had already filled that quota. My apprehension about
the draft had been building for more than a year—since my cousin
and friend Chris was killed in Vietnam on February 19, 1967. It was a

difficult time for my country and a difficult time for me.

Arriving on the bus at Fort Bliss, Texas, for army basic training, I was lonely and scared. I felt certain that I was going to Vietnam as soon as my training was over. What happened to me during those eight weeks at Fort Bliss was transforming. I soon forgot my fears, and now look back on the period from May 15 to July 17, 1968, as eight of the greatest weeks of my life up to that point. I have since tried to determine what was so beneficial about basic training, and I have pinpointed four things:

- For the first time in my life, I consistently went to bed early and got up early

- It was the first time I regularly ate three balanced meals a day

- I ran more miles than I thought possible and performed hard physical training every day

- I prayed more than I ever had before

During that time I was in the best physical condition of my life. Latter-day Saint physiologist Dr. Victor Cline said, "It is almost impossible to feel discouraged while keeping physically active."[1] The *Church News* later added to my understanding with an article that said, "Exercise can counter mental depression. It stimulates certain chemicals in the brain that promote a feeling of well-being."[2] I believe that because I was obeying the Word of Wisdom during basic training, I was feeling the fruits of the Lord's promise in the Doctrine and Covenants: "And all saints who remember to keep and do these sayings, walking in obedience to the commandments, shall receive health in their navel and marrow to their bones; and shall find wisdom and great treasures of knowledge, even hidden treasures; and shall run and not be weary, and shall walk and not faint" (Doctrine and Covenants 89:18-20).

Not only did I feel great, but uplifting ideas also flowed into my mind at a time when I should have been preoccupied with dread. The Holy Ghost was with me and I received the comfort I needed. I have added to my testimony of those four things multiple times since basic training. When I have the self-discipline to control myself physically, I feel the Spirit, and the things I should do in life become clearer to me. When I don't control the physical side, the Spirit leaves, and I am on my own.

Imagine getting a call on a Sunday night from your closest childhood friend whom you haven't seen for many years. He tells you he'll be in town for the next five days on business and would love to get together with you. The only time he has available, however, is during the early morning hours. That night you agree to meet him at 6 AM for breakfast at a nearby restaurant. You're excited to become reacquainted and talk over old times. But your friend never shows up. You are disappointed and worried that you went to the wrong restaurant. That night he calls to explain that he had been too tired to get out of bed, so the two of you agree to meet the following morning. Again, at 6 AM you are in the appointed place, but your friend doesn't show. That night he calls to explain that he had slept in again. "Let's meet tomorrow morning," he says. The same disappointing scene plays out for two more days. And then you get an e-mail from him: "It was really good talking to you. I would love to get together with you the next time I'm in town. Maybe we could go out to breakfast."

Brigham Young said, "Fulfill your contracts and sacredly keep your word."[3] Keeping your word to a friend is a manifestation of what Christ called the second great commandment, to "love thy neighbor as thyself" (Matthew 22:36–39). You probably like to think of yourself as someone who would not break your word to a loved one. Or would you? Consider this hypothetical promise to your closest friend: "Okay, here's the plan for tomorrow. I'm going to get up at 5 AM without punching the snooze button. First, I'll read my scriptures, and then I'll go for a five-mile run, and then come back and write in my journal, and offer a meaningful prayer. Later I am going to visit the sick, do some family history research, call my mother and tell her I love her, and end the day with a well-prepared Family Home Evening lesson."

Do you recognize who the best friend is? You set your alarm, full of promise for the coming day. The next morning, the alarm goes off, and you are so tired that you push the snooze button and give yourself just ten more minutes. Then something strange happens. The pillow begins to whisper in your ear: "It's 5 AM; only fanatics get up this early.

Besides, you have been working so hard that you need a little more rest for today only. Tomorrow you can get up early, and I promise not to call you a fanatic. If you get up now you are going to be so tired all day that you will be in a bad mood. You cannot afford to do this because you have far too many important things to do. If you will sleep until you barely have time to pick up some donuts and get to work, you will be rested."

You try to resist because the pillow said the same thing yesterday. And thus begins and ends the first battle of the day. It is waged between you and a pillow, or should we say, between you and self-discipline. When the snooze alarm goes off, your pillow calls on its ally—your mattress. It flips over and traps you underneath until you finally escape, just in time to stop at the donut shop and get to work. At work you feel drugged and think that you must not have gotten enough sleep. You are so tired that day that you don't get much done. Thank goodness for tomorrow because you are going to get up at 5 AM and get going on that life mission of yours.

If we would not tell our friends a lie, then why would we let ourselves down with repeated lies and broken promises? President Hinckley said: "In all this world there is no substitute for personal integrity. It includes honor. It includes performance. It includes keeping one's word."[4]

## THINGS THAT REQUIRE DISCIPLINE

That near-euphoric state I experienced in basic training at the aptly named Fort Bliss has returned to me several times in my life, as evidenced by these entries from my journal:

**February 10, 1982:** It's paying off. The getting up early, the time with children, the physical exercise is changing my whole attitude. I have seen things in a whole new light, and can feel myself becoming a new person. Isn't it amazing if we halfway try, the Lord blesses us so much it is unbelievable? It seems every day now I'm learning things that I never even dreamed of before. . . . I have found so many opportunities to help friends in the Church since I started my eliminating-procrastination program. I thank my Heavenly Father for the great things he has helped me with. I have set goals for myself that I didn't believe I would ever be interested in trying. Every time I try to do the things the Lord commands me to do, I am immediately blessed.

**May 29, 1983:** Sometimes to get motivated, I must feel total disgust with myself. This is the feeling I have today. I feel very unworthy of all the great blessings I enjoy. I can't believe how quickly I can go from a spiritual high to the opposite. What's so depressing about it is that I know what the problem is: lack of self-control leads to discouragement. It starts off innocently, a little too much to eat, sleep in a little later than needful, put off physical fitness, and suddenly, I have no patience with the kids and feel terrible with myself . . . and I'm right back to the natural man. It's always a challenge to stay motivated enough to read my scriptures in a meaningful way, to get up early, and stay in good physical condition. But I've found that it's a lot easier to keep up the commitment when you have a routine going than to try to start it up again once it's gone. I'm recommitting today to do better. I've found that living the "easy" life today sure makes for a "difficult" life tomorrow.

**June 1, 1983:** Well, my last entry a few days ago found me low and discouraged. Now I feel excited and happy. What is the difference? Again, I have proven to myself what it takes to help me get motivated to action and feeling spiritual.

1. Get up early in the morning
2. Start the day off studying the gospel and planning my day
3. Maintain a physical fitness program
4. Control my appetite
5. Work hard during the day
6. Pray for help

I guess I should have these points engraved on my forehead, because of the number of times I have discovered them and then lost them again. I'm hoping that making this entry will remind me of what I need to do to maintain a spiritual high.

The lesson is clear to me; my physical and spiritual lives are connected. When I have the self-discipline to take care of my physical side, I also nurture my spiritual side and increase my happiness. When

I fail to master myself, I am unhappy and lose the spirit. It is a constant battle. Brigham Young asked, "Now brethren, can we fight against and subdue ourselves? That is the greatest difficulty we ever encountered, and the most arduous warfare we ever engaged in."[5] And in our day, President Thomas S. Monson reminds us, "Eternal life in the kingdom of our Father is your goal, and self-discipline will surely be required if you are to achieve it."[6]

# PHYSICAL BODIES

Heavenly Father has given you a gift called a body to help in your quest for exaltation. It will also be a great test of your integrity and self-discipline. I had a teacher who taught me that the human body was a wonderful machine for which I should be grateful. He told our class, "I want everyone to put both arms out in front of you and lock them in place. Now, I want you to pretend that you need to comb your hair." With my arms locked, that was not possible. Then he said he wanted us to act as if we were feeding ourselves. I couldn't do that either. He then asked, "How many of you have ever been grateful for your elbows?" I had to admit that I had not given much thought to my elbows.

The human body can be likened to a vehicle that will help you reach life's destinations and fulfill your mission. Do you treat your body as well as you would a luxury car? Suppose for a moment that you are offered the perfect job—one that will make you happy and financially comfortable. But, the job requires that you drive an expensive car to represent your company's image. Without the car you cannot have the job, and you must buy the car before you collect your first paycheck. You explain your dilemma to your father and he makes you an offer. He has some money set aside for your inheritance, but he will give it to you now. All he asks is that you buy a car with more long-term value than the one the company suggested. The car he has in mind is a classic and will increase in value if you keep it in mint condition; treat it as you would treat a temple.

At first, you baby the car, but with the passage of time, you grow weary of the time and effort it takes. Before long you forget to change the oil, check the fluid levels, or have it serviced. Several times you don't put it in the garage and you leave windows down during a rainstorm.

You take short cuts at high speeds over rough roads. You eat and drink in the car and spill food on the seats. You squeeze into tight parking places, and soon there are multiple dings in the paint where others opened their doors. Money gets tight so you switch from premium to regular gas. Eventually your car becomes the butt of your jokes. You avoid taking the car where your father might see it because you know you have disappointed him and broken your promise.

Likewise, your Heavenly Father mourns when you mistreat the beautiful body he gave you in order that you could see, hear, smell, taste, think, plan, and achieve. Elder Sterling W. Sill said, "Next to the human spirit the human body is the most marvelous of God's creations."[7] Paul posed a penetrating question when he said, "Know ye not that ye are the temple of God?" (1 Corinthians 3:16). The irony is that many of us would never treat our cars the way we treat our bodies. We can purchase another car, but once this body is gone, there is no new model waiting on the lot.

## SELF-DISCIPLINE

Jared and Melanie, two of my institute students, challenged me to run the distance of a half marathon with them, just the three of us in our own private challenge. I was not excited at all, and never expected to finish our race, but I didn't tell them that. On a hot, humid Labor Day in 2001 we trained by running six miles together. It was one of the hardest things I have ever done in my life. I wanted to give up but was embarrassed to be called a quitter. During the training, I talked about the challenge to other institute students. One of them, Curtis, said he wanted to join us. I trained several times a week to get ready so as not to disappoint my students, but by the morning appointed for our race, all three of them had dropped out. Jared and Melanie went to visit friends that day, and Curtis played football. I decided I would go through with it alone to inflict maximum guilt on them.

I began my run at 5:30 AM. At first I ran around the block thinking I was crazy for even attempting this. Then somewhere within myself I found the energy to keep going, and I ran out of the neighborhood. Suddenly I was not doing it to make those who dropped out feel guilty. I was doing it because I wanted to prove something to myself. As I miraculously neared

163

the completion of my run, I imagined my wife and our two daughters waiting in our driveway to cheer me over the finish line. As I rounded the corner, I saw no fans; they probably didn't expect me back this soon. So I made another slow loop around the block. As my house came into view, I saw my wife come out the front door. For her benefit, I sprinted the last few yards and ended in the driveway, gasping for air.

"Did you run that fast the whole time?" she asked.

"Yeah, right!" I said, "So, did you come out to cheer for me?"

"No. You've been gone so long that I thought something was wrong."

The rest of my cheering section, Natalie and Nichelle, were still in bed.

I learned an important lesson that day. Jared, Melanie, and Curtis did not feel one ounce of guilt that I ran 13.1 miles without them. My wife and daughters didn't really care if I ran that morning either. I learned that you can't count on other people to give you the self-discipline required to take care of your body. That's why it's called "self-discipline" instead of "other-discipline." No one else can give it to you, and it is not for sale. It must come from deep within, and you must do it because you know it will bless your life and help you fulfill your mission.

President Hinckley said, "Be strong—be strong in the discipline of self. How many otherwise good men squander their strength and dissipate their will and literally destroy their lives because they have not the power of self-discipline."[8]

Some people say that they don't have time to exercise. Elder Joe J. Christensen said, "It is easy to rationalize that we don't have time to exercise. Not so. Ultimately, our improved health through exercise will provide us more time and energy to accomplish other tasks. We can usually do about whatever we want to—if we want to badly enough."[9] Stephen R. Covey pointed out that, "Exercising doesn't *take* time. It *saves* time. Still, few consistently do it."[10] A cartoon illustrated the point. It pictured a doctor asking an overweight patient, "Which does fit your schedule better? To exercise for one hour a day, or to be dead twenty-four hours per day?"

A few years ago, a respected Latter-day Saint medical doctor, Larry W. Gibbons, spoke to my Church Educational System group. He was at that time the president and medical director of the Cooper Aerobics Center in Dallas Texas, one of the most respected health and fitness centers in the world. (He later was called to be a General Authority of the Church.) As part of his presentation to our CES group, Dr. Gibbons answered a range of questions. One of our group asked what the doctor knew about President Hinckley's exercise regimen. We learned that the prophet was a regular on the treadmill and used resistance training. How would a man in his mid-nineties travel the world and inspire the Saints if he were a couch potato?

The leaders of our Church live to such advanced ages because the Lord sustains them physically *and* because they take better care of their bodies than other seniors. Church headquarters is populated with men in their 90s who behave as if they were in their 60s. By contrast, our wards are *not* populated with 90-year-old men running Cub Scout programs and teaching the Sunbeams. The typical high priest doesn't live anywhere near to the age of our apostles and prophets. Healthy adherence to the Word of Wisdom and exercise play a huge role in longevity. Consider the following statements from our leaders about lifestyle and how it relates to quality of life:

**Brigham Young (died age 76 when average life expectancy was about 50)** "My mind becomes tired, and perhaps some of yours do. If so, go and exercise your bodies."[11]

**President Spencer W. Kimball (died age 90)** "That is a part of the program—that we will perfect our physical bodies. We will make them just as attractive as possible. We will keep them as healthy as possible. We will keep them in the best condition so far as we can. And so, we will make them like our Lord's."[12]

**President Ezra Taft Benson (died age 94)** "Physical well-being is not only a priceless asset to oneself—it is a heritage to be passed on. With good health, all other activities of life are greatly enhanced. A clean mind in a healthy body enables one to render far more effective service to others. It helps one provide more vigorous leadership. It gives our every experience in life more zest and more meaning. Robust health is a noble and worthwhile attainment."[13]

**President Gordon B. Hinckley (died age 97)** "In brief, a sacred concept is attached to the human body. As such, it ill becomes any man or woman to injure or dissipate his or her health."[14]

**President Marion G. Romney (died age 90)** Elder F. Burton Howard said of him, "Resolving to keep himself physically fit while he was on his mission, regular exercise became a part of his life. With few exceptions and without regard to where he might find himself, he conducted a personally devised physical fitness program every morning throughout the balance of his life. The mission routine soon became part of his life."[15]

**Elder Joseph B. Wirthlin (died age 91)** "Sister Wirthlin is a great example when it comes to exercising. She either plays tennis or walks two miles every day. She often persuades me to go walking with her, and this is no leisurely stroll. Exercise is an important part of our day, and the time spent in it will pay dividends."[16]

# You Need Strength

When I attended my fortieth high school reunion, I was shocked to see the difference between those who had taken care of themselves and those who had not. Many of my classmates looked twenty years older than they actually were and their abilities were severely limited.

If you are to accomplish your life mission, it will require you to be physically and mentally fit. Elder Robert L. Simpson said, "Only those who are physically fit can expect to make the maximum contribution and fulfill his obligation to society as he should."[17] Make an assessment of your current physical state and make the changes necessary to live a vibrant, active, long life—one that will allow you time and energy to complete the tasks you were sent to accomplish.

## Notes

1. Mayola R. Miltenberger, "Happiness: There's Not a Single Barrier," *Ensign*, April 1988, 32.
2. "Each is Responsible for Own Health—Years of Neglect Take Toll in Later Life; Good Lifestyle Pays Dividends," *LDS Church News*, May 4, 1996.
3. Brigham Young, *Discourses of Brigham Young*, 232.
4. Gordon B. Hinckley, *Teachings of Gordon B. Hinckley*, 270.
5. Brigham Young, *Journal of Discourses*, 6:315.
6. Thomas S. Monson, "Pathways to Perfection," *Ensign*, May 2002, 99.
7. Sterling W. Sill, in Conference Report, 1964, 13.
8. Gordon B. Hinckley, "Building Your Tabernacle," *Ensign*, November 1992, 50.
9. Joe J. Christensen, *One Step at a Time: Building a Better Marriage, Family, and You*, 124.
10. Stephen R. Covey, *How to Succeed with People*, 1–2.
11. Young, *Discourses of Brigham Young*, 190.
12. Spencer W. and Edward L. Kimball, *The Teachings of Spencer W. Kimball*, 378.
13. Ezra Taft Benson, *God, Family, Country*, 217.
14. Gordon B. Hinckley, *What of the Mormons?*, 29.
15. F. Burton Howard, *Marion G. Romney: His Life and Faith*, 66.
16. Joseph B. Wirthlin, *Finding Peace in Our Lives*, 226.
17. Robert L. Simpson, in Conference Report, April 1963, 54.

# CHAPTER 18

———❦———

# GO TO BED EARLY
# AND GET UP EARLY

*Let us go to bed early, that we may rise early . . . so far*
*as we can. It is God's plan . . . and we should obey.*
—President Joseph F. Smith

Your most important partner in your quest to discover and accomplish your mission is the Holy Ghost. Over the years I have asked many people this question: "What one piece of advice would you give to help sustain the constant companionship of the Spirit?" Their answers have been useful, if predictable—prayer, fasting, temple attendance, scriptures, good music, service. Only once have I seen the advice that one General Authority, Harold B. Lee, gave to another, Marion G. Romney. Elder Joe J. Christensen retold the story:

> Years ago, Barbara and I had a special opportunity to chauffeur President and Sister Marion G. Romney from Provo to their home in Salt Lake City. Along the way, President Romney shared some of his personal experiences from when he was first called to serve as a General Authority in 1941. He had been serving as a stake president at the time, and had gone to general conference. To his amazement, he was announced and sustained as a new General Authority—an Assistant to the Quorum of the Twelve—without his prior knowledge; no one had talked to him about the calling before the session started. He was shocked and very nervous. He felt that he needed some advice, so he went to Elder Harold B. Lee,

a relatively new member of the Quorum of the Twelve and a former contemporary as a stake president. Elder Romney asked him for advice about how to be successful as a General Authority.

Elder Lee spoke about the necessity of receiving personal revelation in order to be effective and said: "If you are to be successful as a General Authority, you will need to be inspired. You will need to receive revelation. I will give you one piece of advice: *Go to bed early and get up early.* If you do, your body and mind will become rested and then in the quiet of those early morning hours, you will receive more flashes of inspiration and insight than at any other time of the day."

President Romney said: "From that day on, I put that counsel into practice, and I know it works."[1]

"Early to bed and early to rise" is one of the great hidden treasures that few ever discover in this life. Consider the case for going to bed early and getting up early. We have only limited information about Jesus' life. He "went about doing good, and healing all that were oppressed of the devil; for God was with him" (Acts 10:38). But what time did he get up? What time did he go to bed? The following two scriptures give insight into that question. "And in the morning, *rising up a great while before day*, he went out, and departed into a solitary place, and there prayed" (Mark 1:35, emphasis added). We also read, "And *early in the morning* he came again into the temple, and all the people came unto him; and he sat down, and taught them" (John 8:2, emphasis added). If we want to be close to the Savior, we need to do the things he did.

President Boyd K. Packer said, "When I'm under pressure, you won't find me burning the midnight oil. I'd much rather be in bed early and getting up in the wee hours of the morning, when I can be *close to Him who guides this work*."[2] Elder Christensen added his testimony by saying, "Some are habituated to going to bed late and sleeping much longer than your system really needs and thus missing out on some of the *personal inspiration* you could be receiving."[3]

## THREE BOLD PROMISES

In a 1758 publication, Ben Franklin famously opined, "*Early to bed and early to rise*, makes a man *healthy, wealthy* and *wise*."[4] Notice that the three claimed benefits of this practice are among the top things that people worldwide desire. They also may be things that can assist you in accomplishing your life mission. The connection between sleeping habits and the trio of health, wealth, and wisdom has been around for much longer than Franklin's couplet. Aristotle, a Greek philosopher born in 384 BC, said, "It is well to be up *before daybreak*, for such habits contribute to *health, wealth*, and wi*sdom*."[5]

King Solomon in the Old Testament taught the link between prosperity and early rising. He said, "Love not sleep, lest thou *come to poverty*; open thine eyes, and thou shalt be *satisfied with bread*" (Proverbs 20:13, emphasis added).

Samuel Johnson, the Eighteenth Century essayist, poet, and editor, practiced a do-as-I-say-not-as-I-do approach: "I have all my life long been lying in bed till noon; yet I tell all young men, and tell them with great sincerity, that nobody who does not rise early will ever do any good."

# Health

The Lord agrees with Franklin and Aristotle. In Doctrine and Covenants 88:124 we read, "Cease to be idle; cease to be unclean; cease to find fault one with another; cease to sleep longer than is needful; retire to thy bed early, that ye may *not be weary*; arise early, that your *bodies and your minds may be invigorated*."

Defining some terms from the verse enhances the message: "[R]etire to thy bed early, that ye may not be weary [*physically or mentally exhausted*]; arise early, that your bodies and your minds may be invigorated [*filled with life and energy*]."

When the Lord tells us to do something specific in scripture, we call that a commandment. If the Lord's instruction regarding sleep habits is a commandment, then it is one of the commandments most often broken. Yet the promises he makes to those who obey are incredible. Imagine living life without *physical or mental exhaustion* and having your body and mind filled with *life and energy*.

Someone I know of who followed the commandment was the CEO of a major international corporation at ninety-seven years old. He still traveled the world giving talks, training leaders, meeting with heads of state, and being interviewed by major media organizations. His top VPs were eighty-seven and eighty years old respectively, and they also followed the Lord's commandment on sleep habits and kept pace with their boss. That trio was Gordon B. Hinckley, James E. Faust, and Thomas S. Monson. They lived the Word of Wisdom, exercised and added another beneficial behavior—they went to bed early and rose early.

After hearing a General Authority mention during a stake conference that he got up very early every morning, I asked him how many of the First Presidency and Quorum of the Twelve did the same. His eyes locked on mine and he exclaimed, "They all do!"

Going to bed early and getting up early not only will enhance your physical health, but your mental health as well. Many in our society are depressed and spend large sums of money searching for joy, not realizing that "joy cometh in the morning" (Psalms 30:5). Elder Sterling W. Sill said, "To give the journey through life a downhill grade, *get up early enough to watch the sun rise.* It is exciting to experience the light, warmth, and energy that helps to make the earth beautiful with flowers and vegetation."[6] Elder Russell M. Nelson also tied this practice to our mental well being when he said, "To those who feel defeated and downtrodden, look to the early hours of the day for your rescue."[7]

One morning Wendy and I went to the gym before dawn. As we walked home, few people were out, and the world was calm and peaceful. We watched the Sun come over the horizon, and I was filled with gratitude. The challenges of the night before seemed manageable, and I was excited to start the day. If you are to fulfill your mission, good physical and mental health will play a major role.

# WEALTH

A few years ago, Steven, one of our sons-in-law, was having a difficult semester because of extremely challenging science classes. We talked several times about the benefit of going to bed early and getting up early. He took my advice to heart, and one day he called me and excitedly described two commercials he had seen while watching CNN and riding his exercise bike at 5 AM. One was for a Mercedes and the second was for a Jaguar. He wanted to know if I understood the significance. I did, and called one of my sons to see if he got it, too. He quickly replied, "The companies are target marketing successful people. Only rich people are up at 5 AM watching CNN, and the advertisers know it." Contrast that with late-night "infomercials" for cheap gadgets, and ads for weight loss products and job retraining programs. Marketers are like Santa Claus—they know when you are sleeping, and know when you're awake.

Once I asked the CEO of a multi-billion dollar Fortune 500 company to describe his typical day. He said he always got up by 5 AM and tried to go to bed by 10 PM. He began the practice at age nineteen and never stopped. I don't know what time the typical CEO in America rises each morning, but my guess is that it is early. Skeptics will say, "Of course CEOs have to get up early because of their workload." Perhaps the cause and effect goes the other direction—success and its accompanying responsibilities came *because* they were early risers.

While most people are familiar with Benjamin Franklin's maxim, many don't know the full context. He suggests that those who get up late are not likely to become successful and gives the reason: "He that riseth late must trot all day, and shall scarce overtake his business at night; while laziness travels so slowly that *poverty soon overtakes him*. Drive thy business, let not that drive thee; and early to bed and early to rise, makes a man healthy, *wealthy*, and wise."[8]

# WISDOM

The first time I met Adam was when he walked into my office at the institute when I was serving as the director. At first glance, because of his long hair, beard, and sloppy dress, I thought he was one of the homeless guys that occasionally came into the building looking for a handout. I quickly learned, however, that Adam was a returned missionary and a student at the University of Texas in Austin. As we talked, he revealed that he was overwhelmed with school and depressed. He was ready to quit school and give up on his dream of becoming a medical doctor. Since he didn't think he could pass the very difficult premed classes he was taking, he came seeking counsel and a priesthood blessing. After listening to him for a while, I asked if he minded if I spoke boldly. He said he wanted me to be blunt if it would help. It was time for me to ask him the question that almost always prompts the same response from a returned missionary. "What was the happiest time of your life?" It was the two years he had spent as a missionary in the Philippines.

"What time did you get up every morning in the Philippines?"

"6 AM."

"What time did you get up this morning?"

"8:30."

I suggested that if Adam wanted to be successful and overcome his depression, he was going to have to go back on a mission—this time a school mission. My counsel was for him to approach school as he had approached his mission: keep the same schedule, work like a missionary, and look like a missionary. After I gave him a priesthood blessing, he left.

Two days later I walked into the foyer of the Institute building and saw a young man I did not recognize at first. It was Adam. He had shaved, cut his hair, and was neatly dressed. He had begun his "school mission." Adam was later honorably discharged from that mission with a diploma and a 3.90 grade point average. As he followed the counsel of the Lord, Adam became a wise young man. President Boyd K. Packer proclaimed the benefits of keeping an early schedule in school when he said, "I counsel our children to do their critical studying in the *early hours of the morning* when they're fresh and alert, rather than to fight physical weariness and mental exhaustion at night. I've learned the power of the dictum, *'Early to bed, early to rise.'"*[9]

A scientific study conducted by researchers at Brigham Young University in Provo found, "Students who habitually go to bed late and sleep late the next day have lower grade point averages (GPAs) than students with early-to-bed and early-to-rise sleeping habits. The later students slept in the morning, the lower their grades tended to be. Out of all the factors studied, weekday and weekend wakeup times had the strongest association with students' GPAs. Every hour over the average that students slept in on weekdays was associated with a 0.13-point drop on the GPA (0.0–4.0 scale)."[10]

The average college student in America seems to do just the opposite of what this research suggests. A common practice for college students is to stay up until the early morning hours studying, and then they sleep late. At a time when students should be gaining wisdom, many are doing the exact opposite of what will lead to it.

## The Benefits of Getting More Accomplished

The Lord has warned repeatedly in scripture about wasting time:

- "But wo unto him that . . . wasteth the days of his probation, for awful is his state!" (2 Nephi 9:27)
- "Thou shalt not be idle." (Doctrine and Covenants 42:42)
- "Thou shalt not idle away thy time." (Doctrine and Covenants 60:13)

In our fast-paced society, idle time is at a premium. The days of sitting out on the front porch visiting with neighbors are a thing of the distant past. We have more time-saving devices than any other age in history, but our work expands to fill the hours. No wonder the Lord warns us not to idle away the time that we do have. Sleeping is not a waste of time, but sleeping "longer than is needful" would surely be considered idleness. Elder Joe J. Christensen made the following observations: "The world is a more beautiful place early in the morning. Life is so much more calm. *Much more can be accomplished in a shorter amount of time.*"[11]

Experience has taught me that the statement made by Elder Christensen is true. The world really is more beautiful and calm in the early morning hours. Also, when I go to bed early and get up early, I have far more energy and get much more accomplished. I've also found that only the early/early combination works. You cannot follow the early/late, late/early, or the late/late combination and expect the results promised.

President Hinckley's parents taught him to follow the Lord's counsel regarding sleep. In President Hinckley's biography, Sheri L. Dew wrote, "The farm also presented the Hinckley children with opportunities to work. Bryant was typically up by 5:00 AM, and he expected his family to keep an early clock."[12]

One of my favorite teachers at BYU was Cleon Skousen. He had a long list of achievements. One day a student asked him how he got so much accomplished. One of his responses was that he was usually up before sunrise. I remember thinking as a naïve young man that it must be unhealthy to get up that early. Years passed, and I would occasionally see his name linked with an impressive project. I marveled that he was still alive, let alone still working. He died in 2006, just eleven days before his ninety-third birthday, and was still going strong in the years leading up to his death.

# HOW TO DO IT

In our fast-paced world filled with so many activities, going to bed early takes every bit as much willpower as getting up early. Perhaps that is why so few people actually do it. President Joseph F. Smith, writing to one of his missionary sons said, "The Lord said, 'Retire to bed early,' and this is wise advice, *but we do not heed it.* Now let me say, Let us go to bed early, that we may rise early and be refreshed. So far as we can. It is God's plan. He tells us to do it, and *we should obey.*"[13]

Your body has particular sleep needs. An eight-hour sleep cycle may be too much or not enough, and the need may change for you over time. On one extreme, we see people such as Thomas Edison, who needed only four or five hours of sleep a night and kept a breakneck pace the next day. Apparently that worked for him because he lived eighty-four years and acquired an astounding 1,093 patents. Everyone needs to find out how much sleep they need to have an effective day. Experiment to determine the amount your own body needs. Some may think that they are biologically programmed to be a morning person or a night person. But Elder Christensen addressed this when he said, "Nowhere do the scriptures say, 'Thou shalt sleep eight hours.' Nor do they say, 'Retire early unless you happen to be a night person.'"[14]

Any time the natural man tugs at you, it will be a difficult battle to win. Going to bed early and getting up early pose a challenge. Perhaps you can rely on a technique learned in childhood. I never had any trouble getting up early on Christmas Day. Kevin Rollins, former CEO of Dell, told a YSA group why he got up early. "I'm so excited about life that I can't sleep any longer!"

When you prepare for bed tonight, reflect for a few minutes on what will excite you the following day. Then, when the alarm sounds, get up and open your presents, which include physical and mental health, wealth, wisdom, spirituality, happiness, and increased productivity.

---

Notes

1. Joe J. Christensen, *One Step at a Time*, 125.
2. Boyd K. Packer, *Teach Ye Diligently*, 245.
3. "Good Resolutions Make Your Life Happier, Successful," *LDS Church News*, January 15, 1994.
4. Benjamin Franklin, *The Way to Wealth Being the Preface to Poor Richard's Almanac for 1758*.
5. Aristotle, wikipedia.org
6. Sterling W. Sill, *The Wealth of Wisdom*, 144.
7. Russell M. Nelson, "Joy Cometh in the Morning," *Ensign*, November 1986, 67.
8. Benjamin Franklin, *Poor Richard's Almanac*, emphasis added.
9. Packer, *Teach Ye Diligently*, 245.
10. Michelle McKean, "College Students' Academic Stress and Its Relation to Their Anxiety, Time Management, and Leisure Satisfaction," *Journal of American College Health*, 2000; 49: 125–30.
11. Joe J. and Barbara K. Christensen, *Making Your Home a Missionary Training Center*, 34.
12. Sheri L. Dew, *Go Forward with Faith: The Biography of Gordon B. Hinckley*, 26.
13. Hyrum M. Smith III and Scott G. Kenney, comp, *From Prophet to Son: Advice of Joseph F. Smith to His Missionary Sons*, 97, emphasis added.
14. Christensen, *Making Your Home a Missionary Training Center*, 33.

# CHAPTER 19

※

# KEEP A POSITIVE AND CHEERFUL ATTITUDE

*I do not know how anybody can feel gloomy for very long who is a member of this Church. . . . Be positive.*
—President Gordon B. Hinckley

In the ancient world of the Israelites, the oldest son held a place of honor. As the owner of the birthright, he stood to inherit not just the land and possessions of his father, but also the right to preside over the family. Even in the animal kingdom, the firstborn of the flock was considered dedicated to God. Jesus Christ's place among the children of God as the "firstborn" was symbolic of this right of inheritance and dedication to the Lord. In Lehi's family, Laman held that place of honor, and he lost it to his younger brother Nephi because Laman failed to live up to the Lord's expectations for him.

When the time came for Lehi's sons to get the brass plates, "the lot fell upon Laman" (Nephi 3:11). The children of Israel believed that the outcome of casting lots was divinely inspired, thus making this one of the Lord's missions for Laman. The divine influence over this selection process is evidenced by the Apostles using the method of casting lots to fill the vacancy created by Judas Iscariot. (See Acts 1:26.)

What happened that led to Laman's loss of the birthright? He had plenty of opportunities to step up, including the mission involving the brass plates. Laman had the trust of Lehi. He heard the voice of the Lord and saw an angel. These verses give some insight into Laman's fatal flaw:

And thus Laman and Lemuel, being the eldest, did *murmur* against their father. And they did *murmur* because they knew not the dealings of that God who had created them (1 Nephi 2:12, emphasis added).

And it came to pass that I, Nephi, being exceedingly young, nevertheless being large in stature, and also having great desires to know of the mysteries of God, wherefore, I did cry unto the Lord; and behold he did visit me, and did soften my heart that I did believe all the words which had been spoken by my father; wherefore, I did not rebel against him like unto my brothers (1 Nephi 2:16).

And now, behold thy brothers *murmur*, saying it is a hard thing which I have required of them; but behold I have not required it of them, but it is a commandment of the Lord. Therefore go, my son, and *thou shalt be favored of the Lord, because thou hast not murmured*. And it came to pass that I, Nephi, said unto my father: I will go and do the things which the Lord hath commanded, for I know that the Lord giveth no commandments unto the children of men, save he shall prepare a way for them that they may accomplish the thing which he commandeth them (1 Nephi 3:5-7, emphasis added).

Apparently part of the reason for Laman's fall was his murmuring, faultfinding attitude. He therefore lost his birthright and aborted the mission he was sent to do. On the other hand, Nephi had a positive "go and do" attitude about anything the Lord asked of him. Because of this approach, he was favored of the Lord.

The Lord's expectations for his children have not changed since the days of Nephi. He still chooses positive "go and do" people to carry out his great work. All of the prophets in our dispensation have accomplished remarkable things while maintaining upbeat and inspiring attitudes, despite their trials and setbacks. The Lord cannot use those with negative murmuring attitudes to complete his most essential missions. Consider the cheerful attitudes of our last two prophets.

# GORDON B. HINCKLEY

Everyone in the Church has some memory of the wit and humor of President Hinckley and his wife, Marjorie. Speaking at the dedication of the San Antonio Temple, President Hinckley said, "I feel like the last leaf on the tree in the fall with the wind blowing," and "I don't know why the Lord has allowed me to live so long. But let me just say this. At my age, you never buy green bananas!"

Marjorie was once asked to speak to students at the Orem, Utah, Institute. She was short in stature and could barely see over the podium. When she began speaking, she forgot to pull the microphone down and people couldn't hear her. President Hinckley had accompanied her, so he got up and pulled the microphone down. Marjorie stopped speaking and watched him walk back to his seat. She then turned to the audience and said, "That's why I bring him along, for things just like this." They were a couple that had much fun together.

Some of our family had a chance to attend general conference during President Hinckley's term, and we stayed after the proceedings to watch the General Authorities as they left the stand. As President Hinckley walked slowly from the stage, waving his cane in a gesture of farewell to the audience, he came to one of the security men standing at the edge of the stage. He stopped in front of the guard, faced him directly, and then tapped him with the cane, first on the left shoulder and then on the right. The security man bowed as if he had just entered knighthood. President Hinckley shuffled off quickly like a child leaving the scene of a prank, with a huge smile on his face. Here was a man who lived what he taught. He once said, "I do not know how anybody can feel gloomy for very long who is a member of this Church. . . . Be positive."[1]

# Thomas S. Monson

After President Hinckley's death, many Church members wondered if they could ever warm to another prophet. Then came the April 2008 General Conference session where President Thomas S. Monson was sustained. Those who attended the priesthood session later that night would never forget the experience he shared.

I have thought of an experience I had some years ago while attending a stake conference. During the general session, I observed a young boy sitting with his family on the front row of the stake center. I was seated on the stand. As the meeting progressed, I began to notice that if I crossed one leg over the other, the young boy would do the same thing. If I reversed the motion and crossed the other leg, he would follow suit. I would put my hands in my lap, and he would do the same. I rested my chin in my hand, and he also did so. Whatever I did, he would imitate my actions. This continued until the time approached for me to address the congregation. I decided to put him to the test. I looked squarely at him, certain I had his attention, and then I wiggled my ears. He made a vain attempt to do the same, but I had him! He just couldn't quite get his ears to wiggle. He turned to his father, who was sitting next to him, and whispered something to him. He pointed to his ears and then to me. As his father looked in my direction, obviously to see my ears wiggle, I sat solemnly with my arms folded, not moving a muscle. The father glanced back skeptically at his son, who looked slightly defeated. He finally gave me a sheepish grin and shrugged his shoulders."[2]

As President Monson told the story, he wiggled his ears, to the delight of thousands of priesthood holders, some of whom spent time in front of their mirrors that night trying to "follow the prophet." We were no longer thinking of the past but of the bright future, thanks to the positive attitude and playful nature of our new prophet.

## Follow in Line

These two great prophets are following in the footsteps of those who have gone before them. Joseph Smith was an excellent example of being optimistic, and he wanted others to be positive also. He said, "Never get discouraged, whatever difficulties might surround you. If you were sunk in the lowest pit of Nova Scotia, and all the Rocky Mountains piled on top of you, you ought not to be discouraged, but hang on, exercise faith, and keep up good courage and you should come out on top of the heap."[3]

Many of our General Authorities seem to share this upbeat quality of the prophets. They are like Nephi, chosen in part because they have learned not to murmur. Can you envision one of our Apostles today expressing a negative attitude when given an assignment?

"Elder _____, we need you to go to Houston, Texas, next month to create a new stake."

"Houston! Why do I have to go to Houston? I hate the heat, humidity, and mosquitoes. Why do I have to go there? Why can't you give it to Elder_____? No, you always give him the cushy, fun assignments like Hawaii. Just because I'm the junior Apostle doesn't mean that I should be treated like this. I'm tired of it!"

The conversation would not happen because the Lord does not call those with murmuring attitudes to do his important work.

While attending BYU, I heard a talk given by Leonard J. Arrington, who was serving as Church historian at the time. He participated in the "Last Lecture Series," where the speakers were to prepare a talk as if it were the last one they would ever give. The student introducing him said, "Leonard J. Arrington will be our Last Lecture speaker today." Brother Arrington got up and with a twinkle in his eye said, "Last lecture? I thought when you called you said Laugh Lecture, so I prepared a talk on humor." He then proceeded to tell one experience after another about General Authorities and their cheerful, positive attitudes.

I love reading about the inspiring lives of our Church leaders—the men and women who help the work go forward. They look on the bright side of life. I make a habit of writing down experiences they tell about themselves and each other during stake conferences.

When President Spencer W. Kimball was very old, his secretary D. Arthur Haycock was pushing him in his wheelchair through the underground tunnel the General Authorities use to get from the Church Office Building to the Salt Lake Temple. Elder Robert D. Hales, dressed in white, was also in the tunnel. When President Kimball saw him walking toward them, he called Elder Hales over, kissed him on the cheek, and said with a smile, "I thought you were the angel who had come to get me."

Elder LeGrand Richards was on assignment at a stake conference when a man came up to him after his talk and asked, "Do you remember me?" The brethren must get that question often. "Of course, I do," Elder Richards said.

The man put him on the spot and said, "What is my name?"

Elder Richards, unfazed, turned to the regional representative with him and said, "Can you help this man? He can't remember his name." He then went on shaking others' hands.

When Elder Carlos Asay came to visit my stake conference, he shared an experience he had while lying critically ill in the intensive care unit of a hospital. His bishop delivered a box of cards and drawings from the Primary children of Elder Asay's ward. Elder Asay described one of the cards this way: "One young lad drew a picture of me stretched out on a coffin. Protruding out of my chest was a single rose. Off to the side of the sketch were these words: 'Please get well, but if not, have fun!' I laughed so loud and hard that the nurses came rushing into the room, wondering what was wrong. Those moments of humor were lifting to my spirits and, I believe, healing to my body."[4]

## SAY SOMETHING POSITIVE

The story is told about a little boy who didn't talk. His parents tried everything to get him to say his first words, but without success. Through the years they gave up and assumed he would never talk. One day at the dinner table, the boy, then nine years old, suddenly exclaimed, "These potatoes are cold."

The parents were shocked but thrilled. His father said, "Hey, you can talk!"

"Of course, I can talk. I'm nine years old."

The father said, "I don't understand. Why did you wait so long to say your first words?"

"Well, up until now everything was going pretty good."

I think some of us can be a little like this young boy. We don't have much to say unless it's negative. We forget to focus on the many positive things that are happening in our lives.

Every time I attend a funeral, I hear glowing things said about the individual being remembered. I never hear anything like "Bro. \_\_\_\_ was the sorriest, no good rascal that ever lived in these parts." Eulogies always focus on the person's good qualities and not on the faults that we know they had. It is a proper practice, but why wait until a person dies to identify their best qualities?

I learned a valuable lesson from a radio station that had a "Say-Something-Positive-About" program. The host threw out a topic, and listeners were invited to call in and say something positive about it. If the topic was taxes, the callers quickly came up with the benefits of taxation—police protection, fire departments, highways, the military, parks, historical sites, schools, and so on. Before the program ended, I could sense that even the most negative of topics could be seen in a new light.

## Not Outside Influences

In reality, many of our problems are caused by our attitudes about what happens to us. We often see ourselves as victims, instead of agents who are free to act for ourselves in harmony with divine principles. Many expressions common to our everyday communications feed into the notion that our feelings are driven by outside influences. "He makes me so mad!" No, we choose to be so angry. We determine our attitudes by the way we choose to perceive what is happening around us. We can either look on the bright side or choose to have a sour approach to life.

A bad attitude will severely limit how the Lord can use you. You even risk losing your birthright. Elder Neal A. Maxwell once said, "We can learn that at the center of our agency is our freedom to form a healthy attitude toward whatever circumstances we are placed in!"[5] In other words, unhappiness does not come because of what happens to us but how we react to what happens to us.

Pleasant people are a joy to be around. They lift and cheer others. They bring difficult situations into perspective. One pleasant person can radiate good feelings that catch on in a household, office, marketplace, or school. Another can be unpleasant, conveying gloom and contention, with those around him walking on eggshells, hoping not to set him off.

All of us know someone who consistently has a positive attitude. This person does not need to be a General Authority to be cheerful and enjoy life. We have been counseled many times to have a good time. Bishop Victor L. Brown said, "May I suggest that you have fun. Now, it isn't really necessary for me to make this suggestion, is it? The Lord, himself, said 'Man is that he might have joy.'"[6]

I once had a man in my ward named Brother Ayala, who was a

convert to the Church from Colombia and spoke with a strong accent. I never saw him when he wasn't happy and cheerful, even though he had grown up in very poor circumstances. The gospel made him happy, and the Lord was able to use him to do great things. During the production of our stake Christmas program, Brother Ayala walked in with his usual smile, greeting everyone he saw. Some older men sat stone-faced on the sidelines waiting to portray their roles as shepherds *celebrating* the birth of Christ. Brother Ayala walked over to them and said with his beautiful accent, "Hey, shepherds, cheer up and smile. It's Christmas!" This good brother followed President Harold B. Lee's counsel: "I have never believed that in order to be righteous one must be sad-faced and solemn. People approved of the Lord have always been those who have laughed and danced and sung as well as worshiped."[7]

Brother Ayala's message was universal: "Hey, you guys, cheer up and smile! You are members of The Church of Jesus Christ of Latter-day Saints who have been saved to come to earth at this time." We sometimes forget what we are doing here and need the Brother Ayalas of the world to remind us.

## LOOK ON THE BRIGHT SIDE

Several years ago, our youngest son Nolan was on his middle school football team. Being the smallest player on the team didn't give him much playing opportunity. He was a wide receiver on a team that seldom threw the ball. I attended every game of the season, except the last one, when another obligation took precedence. I thought as my family left for the game without me that Nolan would probably catch a pass during the only game I had to miss. When the family returned home, our ten-year-old daughter Naomi ran excitedly to me. "Dad, you should have been there! Nolan almost made a touchdown! It was so close!"

I felt sick that I had missed my son's big moment. "What happened?"

Again she exclaimed, "It was so close!"

I pictured my son's great feat—all seventy-five pounds dragging defenders toward the goal line. "What happened?" I asked again.

"Well, he went out for a pass. The quarterback threw the ball toward him. But a boy on the other team was a lot taller than Nolan, so he caught it."

"Do you mean it was an interception?"

"Yeah, that's what it was."

"I thought you said it was almost a touchdown."

"Well, if Nolan would have caught it and run with it, then it would have been."

I had never thought of an interception as "almost" a touchdown. From a proud sister's point of view, however, that's what it was. She taught me that day that situations that look less than ideal can be viewed from a positive perspective.

A fortune-teller studying the hand of a young man delivered the bad news: "You will be poor and unhappy until you are thirty seven years old." The young man responded, "After that, what will happen? Will I be rich and happy?" The fortune-teller said, "No, you'll still be poor, but you'll be used to it by then." The key to a good attitude is to accept the difficulties in life that come to you. Trials and tribulations are inevitable; being miserable is optional.

## Our Responsibility

To fill your divine destiny, you cannot have a negative attitude. You must have a "go and do" positive attitude to make it happen. President Ezra Taft Benson said of your generation, "You are to be the royal army of the Lord in the last days. You are youth of the noble birthright."[8] Many to whom that talk was given are no longer youth. But the fact remains that they are the only army the Lord has, and they do have a noble birthright. Don't squander it with a murmuring, negative attitude as Laman did.

President Kimball said, "I remind you . . . that regardless of your present age, you are building your life; it will be cheap and shoddy or it will be valuable and beautiful; it will be full of constructive activities or it can be destructive; it can be full of joy and happiness, or it can be full of misery. It all depends upon you and your attitudes, for your altitude, or the height you climb, is dependent upon your attitude or your response to situations."[9]

Notes

1. Gordon B. Hinckley, "Words of the Prophet: the Spirit of Optimism," *New Era*, July 2001, 4.
2. Thomas S. Monson, "Examples of Righteousness," *Ensign*, May 2008, 66.
3. Zora Smith Jarvis, *George A. Smith Family*, 54.
4. Carlos Asay, *Family Pecan Trees: Planting a Legacy of Faith at Home*, 100.
5. Neal A. Maxwell, *Deposition of a Disciple*, 30–31.
6. Victor L. Brown, "Is There Balance In Our Lives?" *BYU Speeches of the Year*, May 19, 1964, 3.
7. Clyde J. Williams, ed., *Teachings of Harold B. Lee: Eleventh President of The Church of Jesus Christ of Latter-day Saints*, 621.
8. Ezra Taft Benson, "To the Youth of the Noble Birthright," *Ensign*, May 1986, 43.
9. Spencer W. Kimball, "The Davids and the Goliaths," in Conference Report, October 1974, 112–13.

CHAPTER 20

# RECORD THE
# LESSONS YOU LEARN

*Behold, there shall be a record kept among you.*
—Doctrine and Covenants 21:1

On Sunday, June 25, 2000, I drove to a small cemetery hoping to receive some inspiration for a talk that I was to give that night at the Orange, Texas, Stake Center. Sitting next to my great grandparents' tombstones, I reviewed their lives. William and Joissine Williamson had been baptized into the Church in the spring of 1900. One hundred years later their descendants were commemorating this milestone as a part of the annual Williamson family reunion. I had been asked to offer one of the talks at a fireside that would be held that night in their honor, and I was still unsure of what to say. I knew the stake center would be filled to capacity with their descendants, which now numbered in the thousands.

The tombstone marker included a list of their fifteen children, including birth and death dates. As I glanced over the names, I contemplated the heartache this couple went through as five of their first ten children died young. I wondered how they endured when number fourteen also died. And yet Joissine put her life and mental health to the test again to have child number fifteen––my grandmother Epsie, who was baptized at age eighteen, just months after her parents joined the Church in 1900. Gazing at this final resting place for these great people, I felt tremendous love for what they had done for their descendants. I reflected upon the courageous decision they made to join the Church, and I said aloud, "Well Grandpa, what do you want me to say to your descendants tonight?"

After a moment, a voice came into my mind that said, "Tell them that I'm sorry." That was not exactly what I expected to hear. We were celebrating the one hundredth anniversary of William's baptism in a building packed with his descendants, and he wanted me to tell them he was sorry. In my mind I continued my silent conversation, "If you only realized how much we appreciate what you have done for us. Look at how many of your descendants served missions and filled Church leadership positions because of your decision. Why would you be sorry?"

The little voice whispered back. "Tell them I'm sorry for not keeping a journal of my life so that you could read about the events surrounding our baptisms. Tell them I'm sorry for not taking the time to write down who my father was and for the thousands of hours and dollars my descendants have spent looking for him. Ask them not to make the same mistake I did." Then the whispering stopped. That night I shared his message with his descendants in attendance at the fireside. I have no idea how many descendants accepted his challenge to keep a journal of their lives, but I did what he asked me to do. Of course, I recorded the experience in my journal.

President Spencer W. Kimball made it clear that keeping a journal is a commandment from God: "For those of you who may not have already started your books of remembrance and your records, we would suggest that this very day you begin to write your records quite fully and completely. We hope that you will do this, our brothers and sisters, for this is what the *Lord has commanded*."[1] Notice that he didn't say "It would be nice if," or "Would you please consider," or "I suggest that" you keep a journal. The words of the prophet are plain when he said that the Lord "has commanded."

We are not offered all the reasons why this commandment was given, but I have learned, as perhaps you have, that I forget things very quickly when I don't write them down. No wonder the Lord, at the beginning of this dispensation, said, "Behold, there shall be a record kept among you" (Doctrine and Covenants 21:1).

What if Thomas Edison had failed to record what he learned in his quest to invent the electric light? As he moved through hundreds of trial-and-error experiments, it was essential to record the results. We have the technological advances of our day that help bless our lives and spread the gospel because those with life missions studied the lessons of the experts in their fields. They then built upon the previous generations' knowledge, adding key blocks for the next generation to build on. If they had not recorded the lessons they learned along the way, we still would be trying to reinvent the wheel with each new generation. Imagine an Einstein, Newton, or Edison taking what they discovered to the grave.

And yet that is what 99.9 percent of the world's population does. Thus, the majority of humankind cannot learn from the experiences of their fifth great grandparents, or from their immediate family, or even their own life story. In 1862, an article appeared in the territorial newspaper in Utah making the best case that I have ever read for keeping a journal: "If man keeps no diary, the path crumbles away behind him as his feet leave it; and days gone by are but little more than a blank, broken by a few distorted shadows. *His life is all confined within the limits of today.*"[2]

My dad used to use this phrase when he couldn't remember something: "I don't know whether I found a rope or lost a horse!" My father, like the vast majority of those who have ever lived on earth, never kept a journal. All I have from his life are my memories and a few of the stories he shared from before I was born. My children had far fewer memories of him. Now his great grandchildren will only know him through a few embellished stories and a tombstone marker. They will know little about this faithful member of the Church who considered himself too busy to write down what mission he filled in life and what lessons he learned from it.

Others, like my father, who left no account for posterity, had their reasons. Perhaps they also thought they were too busy, or maybe their lives seemed mundane, not worthy of note. More likely, they felt they did not know how to write well enough to express themselves without embarrassment. Those excuses are easily deconstructed.

# Don't Have Time

It is sometimes hard to find time to do everything that needs to be done. And yet you live in an age with more time-saving devices than at any time in history. You probably have dishwashers, microwaves, cars, washing machines and dryers, cell phones, and other modern conveniences, and still there are not enough hours in the day. Americans find time to watch an average of twenty-eight hours of TV per week. Our society finds time to surf the Internet for hours, play video games, and go to the movies and ballgames.

Is the reason our prophets found the time to keep their journals because they didn't have much else to do? President Kimball, for example, most likely was not as busy as you are, because he said, "By now, in my own personal history, I have managed to fill seventy-eight large volumes, which are my personal journal. There have been times when I have been so tired at the end of a day that the effort could hardly be managed, but I am so grateful that I have not let slip away from me and my posterity those things which needed to be recorded."[3]

What Joseph Smith accomplished during the thirty-eight short years before he was killed is incomprehensible. It seems humanly impossible that a person that young could have accomplished what he did in just a little over twenty years from the time he first received the plates until his death. And yet somehow he pulled it off in the midst of tremendous persecution. Brigham Young said of Joseph's life, "He passed a short life of sorrow and trouble, surrounded by enemies who sought day and night to destroy him. If a thousand hounds were on this Temple Block, let loose on one rabbit, it would not be a bad illustration of the situation at times of the Prophet Joseph. He was hunted unremittingly."[4]

If anyone did not have time to keep a journal, it was Joseph. And yet he had a tremendous desire to record the details of the mission the Lord sent him to accomplish. He wrote of his dissatisfaction with his own journal:

> Since I have been engaged in laying the foundation of The Church of Jesus Christ of Latter-day Saints, I have been prevented in various ways from continuing my journal and

history in a manner satisfactory to myself or in justice to the cause. Long imprisonments, vexatious and long-continued lawsuits, the treachery of some of my clerks, the death of others, and the poverty of myself and brethren from continued plunder and driving, have prevented my handing down to posterity a connected memorandum of events *desirable to all lovers of truth; yet I have continued to keep up a journal* in the best manner my circumstances would allow, and dictate for my history from time to time, as I have had opportunity so that the labors and suffering of the first Elders and Saints of this last kingdom *might not wholly be lost to the world.*[5]

One day you will stand before the judgment bar of God. I don't know every person who will be there with you, but you can count on at least a few journal keepers to be in attendance. Nephi will be there, since he stated, *"You and I* shall stand face to face before Christ's bar" (2 Nephi 33:11, emphasis added). He will be joined by his brother Jacob who wrote in his journal, "Farewell, until I shall *meet you* before the pleasing bar" (Jacob 6:13, emphasis added). One of Nephi's direct descendants Moroni wrote in the last paragraph of his journal, "And now I bid unto all, farewell. I soon go to rest in the paradise of God, until my spirit and body shall again reunite, and I am brought forth triumphant through the air, to *meet you* before the pleasing bar of the great Jehovah, the Eternal Judge of both quick and dead. Amen" (Moroni 10:34, emphasis added).

There may be even more people at our judgment than these great Book of Mormon record keepers. Brigham Young said, "Joseph Smith holds the keys of this last dispensation, and is now engaged behind the veil in the great work of the last days. . . . No man or woman in this dispensation will ever enter into the celestial kingdom of God without the consent of Joseph Smith."[6]

If I don't keep a record of my life I sure hope President Hinckley won't be there since he said, "To you . . . who are old or young, may I suggest that you write, that you keep journals, that you express your thoughts on paper. . . . It will assist you in various ways, and you will bless the lives of many—your families and others—now and in the years to come, as you put on paper some of your experiences."[7]

Finally, I wonder if one of the great journal keepers of our day,

President Thomas S. Monson, will be there. He has kept a detailed journal of his entire ministry, and the Church members eagerly await his retelling of his experiences. I have heard Church members exclaim, "How does he remember all of those experiences from so long ago? He obviously has a photographic memory!" Or there is another possibility: he who keeps a journal doesn't need a photographic memory.

## NOTHING INTERESTING HAS HAPPENED

Another reason for not keeping a journal is that life is boring and there is nothing to record. Those who utter these words badly need to discover what their life mission is. How can we be sent at this critical time of the earth's history, during the years leading up to the Lord's Second Coming, and have a boring life? Nephi did not have a remarkable spiritual experience every day of his life, but he did record events as they happened. His journal did not start off as scripture. Elder Theodore M. Burton observed, "Much of what we now regard as scripture was not anything more or less than men writing of their own spiritual experiences for the benefit of their posterity. These scriptures are family records. Therefore, as a people we ought to write of our own lives and our own experiences to form a sacred record for our descendants. We must provide for them the uplifting, faith-promoting strength that the ancient scriptures now give us."[8]

Your descendants will someday treat your life story as a sacred gift. The day the Lord sent you to earth, you parachuted behind enemy lines to perform a critical mission at a critical time during a world war against evil. You cannot truthfully say that nothing of note happened after you landed on the ground.

Harvey Cluff was born in Kirtland, Ohio, in 1836 to Latter-day Saint converts. He was never an apostle or a prophet. He was sent to earth to live an ordinary life like yours. He spent twenty-five years of his life on missions for the Church. It was nothing special. But he managed to keep a record of that ordinary life and left a message for you in his journal. "No intelligent person in youth or old age should merely drift along. Look the world squarely in the face, listen and learn and not pass along, in life, indifferently, for there are grand lessons before you every minute. Don't let it be said of you that life has been a failure. The royal path of life has been marked out for you by Jesus Christ himself. He that walketh therein, builds upon the foundation that withstands the winds and floods."[9]

## "I'M NOT A GOOD WRITER"

Your journal may not be great literature, but it will be a great treasure because it is in your own words, however humbly or awkwardly you form them. If you have ever read the journal of an ancestor, you already know how endearing their patterns of writing, spelling, and punctuation become to you as you read their sincere words. Get past the notion that you can't write. Put the first words on paper as if you were telling your story around the dinner table, and more words will flow. The Lord will not accept writer's block as an excuse.

## BENEFITS OF JOURNALS

Journals have multiple benefits, not only for your posterity, but also for the here and now. Your journal has the power to change and direct your own life today. It can heal and lift. Personal journals can be your companions in pondering the Lord's hand in your life. Following are the benefits that I know from personal experience to be true.

## ANSWERS FOR DECISIONS

Many times I have found answers to questions or problems in journal entries that I had forgotten about. Joseph Smith spoke of this when he said:

> If I now had in my possession, every decision which had been had upon important items of doctrine and duties since the commencement of this work, I would not part with them for any sum of money; but we have neglected to take minutes of such things, thinking, perhaps, that they would never benefit us afterwards; which, if we had them now, would decide almost every point of doctrine which might be agitated. But this has been neglected, and now we cannot bear record to the Church and to the world, of the great and glorious manifestations which

have been made to us with that degree of power and authority we otherwise could, if we now had these things to publish abroad. . . . For neglecting to write these things when God had revealed them, not esteeming them of sufficient worth, the Spirit may withdraw, and God may be angry; and there is, or was, a vast knowledge, of infinite importance, which is now lost."[10]

One mission president I knew had been an executive with the Marriott Corporation. He said that in an executive meeting, he and others discussed individuals to fill an important position in the company. When a certain man's name was mentioned, someone said, "Well, he does have twenty years of experience." Another quickly pointed out, "No, he has one year of experience repeated nineteen times." The man had not learned enough from his twenty years, and was passed over for the promotion.

## PROTECTION

Without a doubt, the quickest way to have your personal life mission aborted and given to another is through sin. Your journal can be a tool to help you keep account of your actions. Knowing you will record those actions for future generations of readers is a powerful incentive to choose the right. Ask yourself, "Will I feel comfortable recording what I am about to do?" Imagine recording the following events for future generations:

*   This marks the beginning of a new month. It has now been eight months since I have done my home teaching.

*   We went to see an R-rated movie today. It had tons of violence, sex, and profanity, but it was okay, because it taught some valuable lessons.

*   Today at the office party, I drank a beer. I know I shouldn't have, but I don't think one beer is going to hurt anything.

*   My daughter looked so cute tonight when she left for the prom. She is only fourteen, but she got invited by a really nice senior, so we decided that it would be fine just this once.

• I got kicked out of the Church basketball game today for fighting and using a little profanity, but it wasn't my fault. The referee just overreacted.

I could go on, but you get the picture. If you would not feel comfortable writing what you are about to do in your journal for your children and grandchildren to read, then DON'T DO IT! Elder Andrew Jenson, a faithful nineteenth century journal keeper, expounded on this protective value: "The keeping of a journal has a tendency to keep both mind and body on the straight and narrow path. If we keep a journal we naturally desire to write something that will read well. We want to make a good record of ourselves. But in order to do so we must live a good and useful life, and thus by our actions produce materials for a clean and interesting record. We might falsify our records, but, as record makers we would constantly think of the recording angel who is making a true history of all our actions; and if we felt convinced that our record did not correspond with his in the main, we should not feel comfortable."[11]

## JUDGED OUT OF THE BOOKS

John the Revelator saw in vision the judgment bar. He said, "And I saw the dead, small and great, stand before God; and the books were opened: and another book was opened, which is the book of life: and the dead were judged out of those things which were written in the books, according to their works" (Revelation 20:12). I want to make sure that I have an accurate "book" of my life. The last thing I want to do is draw a blank when the Lord asks me what I learned in life: "Hmm. I can't remember."

An editorial from the *Millennial Star* described that moment when the Lord will ask you for an accounting:

Do you keep a Journal? If so, well—and you will have your reward; and if not, we would again enjoin it upon you, and upon all who have not before heard the admonition, to commence forthwith to keep a Journal, or write a history; and see to it, that what you write is strictly true and unexaggerated; so that in the end, all may know of all things concerning this last work, and all knowledge may flow together from the four quarters of the earth, when the Lord shall make his appearing, and we all may be ready to *give a full account of our mission, our ministry and stewardship*, and receive the welcome tidings, "Thou hast been faithful over a few things, I will make thee ruler over many things: enter thou into the joy of thy Lord."[12]

Notes

1. Spencer W. Kimball, "We Need a Listening Ear," *Ensign*, November 1979, 4.
2. "Concerning Hurry and Leisure," *Frazier's Magazine for Town and Country*, vol. LX, July to December 1859, 147.
3. JoAnn Jolley, "The World Conference on Records: Writing the History of the Heart," *Ensign*, October 1980, 72.
4. Brigham Young, *Journal of Discourses*, 10:315.
5. B.H. Roberts, comp., Joseph Smith, journal entry, December 11, 1841, *History of the Church*, 4:470, emphasis added.
6. Young, *Journal of Discourses*, 7:289.
7. Gordon B. Hinckley, "If Thou Art Faithful, *Ensign*, November 1984, 89.
8. Theodore M. Burton, "The Inspiration of a Family Record," *Ensign*, January 1977, 17.
9. Harvey Cluff, *Harvey Cluff, Autobiography*, 8.
10. Joseph Fielding Smith, comp., *Teachings of the Prophet Joseph Smith*, 72–73.
11. Andrew Jenson, "History and Genealogy Discourse," tenth ward meeting house, Sunday evening, January 20, 1895.
12. Parley P. Pratt, ed. "Do You Keep a Journal?" *The Latter-Day Saints Millennial Star*, vol. 1, no. 6, 160.

# ON TO VICTORY

*"Brethren, shall we not go on in so great a cause? Go forward and
not backward. Courage, brethren; and on, on to the victory!"*

—Joseph Smith

One of the great stories in all of scripture relates the conversion of
thousands during the mission of Ammon, Aaron, Omner, and
Himni to the Lamanites. When these four sons of King Mosiah told
their community in Zarahemla of the strong desire they felt to preach
the gospel to the enemy, they were "laughed . . . to scorn" (Alma 26:23).
Their detractors did not stop by just laughing; they also predicted that
the mission would fail. Friends and neighbors, fellow believers, cast
doubt in the minds of the four young men to discourage them from
embarking on their assignment. The doubters said that there was no way
to "bring the Lamanites to the knowledge of the truth" or to convince
them "of the incorrectness of the traditions of their fathers" (Alma
26:24). The energy of the foursome would be better spent destroying
the Lamanites instead of trying to save them. However, these young
men were led by the Lord and had faith enough to plan for success.

Many of you have and will experience similar resistance from
those who should be supportive as you "go and do the things which the
Lord hath commanded" (1 Nephi 3:7). Not everyone will want you to
succeed. You cannot let others' words or actions determine what your
mission will be. That is between you and the Lord.

X As was the case with the sons of Mosiah, the Lord will allow your faith to be tested to the limit to see if you are serious. Ammon said that he and his brothers became so discouraged at one point that they were ready to abandon their mission and turn back. They prayed and received the encouragement they needed to continue. Ammon related what to do when discouragement is about to overcome you: "Now when our hearts were depressed, and we were about to turn back, behold, the Lord comforted us, and said: Go amongst thy brethren, the Lamanites, and bear with patience thine afflictions, and I will give unto you success" (Alma 26:27). *some errands, bring your greatest weaknesses to surface but you must keep trying*

Just because you are on an "errand from the Lord" (Jacob 1:17) does not mean your tasks will all be easy. When these missionaries turned to the Lord, he gave them the courage to face the trials that plagued them during their fourteen-year mission. Surely he will do the same for you. *We must Trust in the Lord*

President Monson reminded us that, "Faith forged in the furnace of trials and tears is marked by trust and testimony."[1] Ammon and his brothers experienced this furnace of trials. He recounts, "And we have been cast out, and mocked, and spit upon, and smote upon our cheeks; and we have been stoned, and taken and bound with strong cords, and cast into prison; and through the power and wisdom of God we have been delivered again" (Alma 26:29). *faith & hope.*

The sons of Mosiah knew they were on a mission for the Lord and were willing to suffer so that "perhaps we might be the means of saving some soul" (Alma 26:30). What would the results have been if Ammon, Aaron, Omner, and Himni had let the mocking of their friends talk them out of the Lamanite mission before they even began? What if the missionaries had listened to their own fears and returned to Zarahemla when they became depressed? If they had turned back, there would have been no:

- Miraculous story of Ammon defending the flocks of King Lamoni.

- Conversion of Lamoni and his guards and his entire household

- Conversion of Lamoni's father and his household

- Two thousand stripling warriors who were taught by their mothers not to doubt

- No burying of their weapons of war by thousands of Lamanite converts.

*or given up*

If the missionaries had turned back, *or given up* the Book of Mormon would be missing some of its most inspiring stories. Would Ammon and his brothers have returned to their old ways had they turned back and not completed their missions? We will never know the answer to that question, but we do know that their father was worried about the possibility. King Mosiah said, "And if my son should turn again to his pride and vain things he would recall the things which he had said, and claim his right to the kingdom, which would cause him and also this people to commit much sin" (Mosiah 29:9).

Fortunately the sons of Mosiah felt the workings of the Spirit so strongly that they did not turn back, *or give up,* and they completed their mission. They had remembered the Lord's kindness toward them and wanted to show their gratitude for being forgiven. "And thus did the Spirit of the Lord work upon them, for they were the very vilest of sinners. And the Lord saw fit in his infinite mercy to spare them; nevertheless they suffered much anguish of soul because of their iniquities, suffering much and fearing that they should be cast off forever" (Mosiah 28:4).

Because they went forward with faith, they felt the joy of victory. Ammon described the feeling that comes when a mission is successfully completed: "Now have we not reason to rejoice? Yea, I say unto you, there never were men that had so great reason to rejoice as we, since the world began; yea, and my joy is carried away . . . " (Alma 26:35).

Because they stayed steadfast and sure, thousands were converted to the truth in their day, and now millions have been inspired by their story in our day. All too often we feel motivated to accomplish something of great importance, but we soon abandon the mission before it even begins. Or we turn back before it is completed and miss the joy that could have been ours. Why is that?

## Too Young and Inexperienced

The adversary will do anything in his power to convince you not to begin or fulfill your life mission. He will send those to mock you and, in the guise of concern, try to talk you out of fulfilling your mission. He will feed on your discouragement so you will choose to turn back. Perhaps he will even whisper that you are incapable of achieving your goals because you do not have the intellect or talent to succeed. Or maybe he will try to convince you that you are too young and inexperienced or too old to do anything of significance.

Joseph Smith was *not* called to be a prophet at the age of thirty-eight. He was called to lay down his life for the cause at thirty-eight, *having already completed* his earthly mission. He taught us that no one is too young or inexperienced to accomplish great things when the Lord is involved. Like the sons of Mosiah, Joseph was surrounded by those who were, in his words, "persecuting me, reviling me, and speaking all manner of evil against me falsely."[2] What if he had listened to the laughing and mocking of those around him when he told them about his mission? What if he had turned back when he became discouraged while in the Liberty Jail?

Joseph did just what the sons of Mosiah did when things looked bleak. He turned to the Lord: "O God, where art thou? And where is the pavilion that covereth thy hiding place?" (Doctrine and Covenants 121:1). After this trial of his faith, the Lord spoke to him and told him to "hold on thy way, and the priesthood shall remain with thee . . ." (Doctrine and Covenants 122:9). Surely the Lord will do the same for you if you will turn to him, no matter your age or education or status among your peers.

## Too Old

Gordon B. Hinckley was not sustained to be the prophet until he was eighty-five years old. In our society, most people retire between sixty-two and sixty-five years of age. Many have either passed away by age eighty-five or reside in assisted-living homes. Some people in the world laugh at and mock the ages of the men the Lord chooses to preside over his Church. President Hinckley was still traveling the world and speaking at general conference when he was ninety-seven years old.

You have clear messages from the sons of Mosiah, the Prophet Joseph Smith, and President Gordon B. Hinckley. If you are on the Lord's errand, he will make up for any limitations you might have. It doesn't matter if you are old or young, brilliant or average, former sinner, or always a saint. The Lord can and will make up for anything that is lacking. As Elder Neal A. Maxwell once said, "God does not begin by asking us about our ability, but only about our availability, and if we then prove our dependability, he will increase our capability!"[3]

## OUR OWN MISSIONS

We *all* have a unique mission to perform on earth. You have not been sent merely to be cheerleaders for others, although you may be called upon to do that, too. Once you discover what your mission is, you must move forward to accomplish it. Those around you may or may not be supportive, but you will have the support of him who matters most.

There is one more important lesson to learn. Do not turn back, no matter how difficult the task becomes. Move forward with courage against whatever obstacle may be placed in your path. Be steadfast and sure, knowing that the Lord has called you to perform a special mission and that he *will* stand by you as you strive to achieve it.

Less than two years before Joseph Smith completed his life mission, he wrote a letter to the members of The Church of Jesus Christ of Latter-day Saints. It is a message that you should take to heart as you go forward with faith: "Brethren, shall we not go on in so great a cause? Go forward and not backward. Courage, brethren; and on, on to the victory! Let your hearts rejoice, and be exceedingly glad" (Doctrine and Covenants 128:22).

Notes

1. Thomas S. Monson, "Tears, Trials, Trust, Testimony," *Ensign*, May 1987, 42.
2. Joseph Smith, *Joseph Smith History*, 1:25.
3. Neal A. Maxwell, "It's Service, Not Status, That Counts," *Ensign*, July 1975, 5.

# BIBLIOGRAPHY

*The American Heritage Dictionary of the English Language.* 4th ed. Chicago: Houghton Mifflin Company, 2000.

Anderson, James H. "The Salt Lake Temple." *Contributor.* April 6, 1893, 243.

Aristotle. wikipedia.org.

———. wiki.wsmoak.net.

Asay, Carlos. *Family Pecan Trees: Planting a Legacy of Faith at Home.* Salt Lake City: Deseret Book, 1992.

Ashton, Marvin J. "A Time of Urgency." In Conference Report. April 1974, 49.

———. "Straightway." *Ensign.* May 1983, 30.

Ballard, M. Russell. "Hyrum Smith: 'Firm as the Pillars of Heaven'." *Ensign.* November 1995, 6.

Beck, Julie B. "What Latter-day Saint Women Do Best: Stand Strong and Immovable." *Ensign,* November 2007, 109–12.

Bennett, William J. "Inertia." *Ensign.* May 1974, 33.

Benson, Ezra Taft. "A Message to the Rising Generation." *Ensign.* November 1977, 30.

———. "Do Not Despair." *Ensign.* October 1986, 5.

———. *God, Family, Country.* Salt Lake City: Deseret Book, 1975.

———. "In His Steps." Church Educational System devotional, Anaheim, California, February 8, 1987.

———. *The Teachings of Ezra Taft Benson.* Salt Lake City: Bookcraft, 1988.

———. *Title of Liberty.* Salt Lake City: Deseret Book, 1964.

———. "To the Young Women of the Church." *Ensign.* November 1986, 81.

———. "To the Youth of the Noble Birthright." *Ensign.* May 1986, 43.

Berra, Yogi. quotationspage.com.

Britsch, R. Lanier. *From the East: The History of the Latter-day Saints in Asia, 1851-1996*. Salt Lake City: Deseret Book, 1998.

Brown, Victor L. "Is There Balance in Our Lives?" *BYU Speeches of the Year*. May 19, 1964.

Burton, Theodore M. "Salvation for the Dead—A Missionary Activity." *Ensign*. May 1975, 69.

———. "The Inspiration of a Family Record." *Ensign*. January 1977, 17.

Chamberlain, Jonathan. *Eliminating Your SDB's: Self-Defeating Behaviors*. Provo, Utah: Brigham Young University Press, 1978.

Christensen, Joe J. *One Step at a Time: Building a Better Marriage, Family, and You*. Salt Lake City: Deseret Book, 1996.

———, and Barbara K. *Making Your Home a Missionary Training Center*. Salt Lake City: Deseret Book, 1985.

Cluff, Harvey. *Harvey Cluff, Autobiography*. BYU Special Collections: Writings of Early Latter-day Saints.

"Concerning Hurry and Leisure." *Frazier's Magazine for Town and Country*. Vol. LX, July to December 1859. London: John W. Parker and Son, West Strand.

Covey, Stephen R. leadernetwork.org.

———. quotationcollection.com.

———. *Spiritual Roots of Human Relations*. Salt Lake City: Deseret Book, 1970.

———. *How to Succeed with People*. Salt Lake City: Deseret Book, 1971.

Cowdery, Oliver. *Times and Seasons*. Vol. 2, no. 1, November 1, 1840, 201.

de Saint Exupéry, Antoine. poetry2share.proboards79.com.

Derrick, Royden G. "The Way to Perfection." *Ensign*. May 1989, 76.

Dew, Sheri L. *Go Forward With Faith: The Biography of Gordon B. Hinckley*. Salt Lake City: Deseret Book, 1996.

"Each Is Responsible for Own Health—Years of Neglect Take Toll in Later Life; Good Lifestyle Pays Dividends." *LDS Church News*. May 4, 1996.

Edison, Thomas. quotationspage.com.

———. worldofinspiration.com.

Emerson, Ralph Waldo. wiki.wsmoak.net.

*Encyclopedia of Mormonism*. Edited by Daniel H. Ludlow. 5 vols. New York: Macmillan, 1992.

Eyring, Henry B. "Do Not Delay." *Ensign*. November 1999, 33.

Faust, James E. "What It Means to Be a Daughter of God." *Ensign*. November 1999, 100.

Featherstone, Vaughn J. *The Incomparable Christ: Our Master and Model.* Salt Lake City: Deseret Book, 1995.

Ford, Henry. quoteworld.org.

*Forever Friends.* Edited by Randal A. Wright. Salt Lake City: Bookcraft 1996.

*For the Strength of Youth: Fulfilling our Duty to God.* Salt Lake City: Intellectual Reserve, 2001.

Franklin, Benjamin. *Poor Richard's Almanac.* October 1750.

———. *The Way to Wealth Being the Preface to Poor Richard's Almanac for 1758.*

"Good Resolutions Can Make Your Life Happier, Successful." *LDS Church News.* January 15, 1994.

Grant, Heber J. "The Nobility of Labor." *Ensign,* March 1972, 67.

Hinckley, Bryant S. *Sermons and Missionary Services of Melvin Joseph Ballard.* Salt Lake City: Deseret Book, 1949.

Hinckley, Gordon B. "Articles of Belief." Bonneville International Corporation Management Seminar, February 10, 1991.

———. "Building Your Tabernacle." *Ensign.* November 1992, 50.

———. "If Thou Art Faithful." *Ensign.* November 1984, 89.

———. "Our Testimony to the World." *Ensign.* May 1997, 83.

———. "The Church Goes Forward." *Ensign.* May 2002, 4.

———. *The Teachings of Gordon B. Hinckley.* Salt Lake City: Deseret Book, 1997.

———. "Watch the Switches in Your Life." *Ensign.* January 1973, 91.

———. *What of the Mormons?* Salt Lake City: Church of Jesus Christ of Latter-day Saints, 1947.

———. "Words of the Prophet: The Spirit of Optimism," *New Era.* July 2001, 4.

Holland, Jeffrey R. "President Gordon B. Hinckley: Stalwart and Brave He Stands." *Ensign,* June 1995, 8.

Howard, F. Burton. *Marion G. Romney: His Life and Faith.* Salt Lake City: Bookcraft, 1988.

Hunter, Howard W. "Bind on Thy Sandals." *Ensign.* May 1978, 34.

*Hymns of the Church of Jesus Christ of Latter-day Saints.* Salt Lake City: The Church of Jesus Christ of Latter-day Saints, 1985.

Jarvis, Zora Smith. *George A. Smith Family.* Provo, Utah: Brigham Young University Press, 1962.

Jefferson, Thomas. quotationspage.com.

Jenson, Andrew. "History and Genealogy Discourse," Tenth Ward meeting house, Sunday evening, January 20, 1895.

Jolley, JoAnn. "The World Conference on Records: Writing the History of the Heart," in News of the Church. *Ensign*. October 1980, 72.

Keller, Helen. goodreads.com.

Kimball, Edward L., and Andrew E. Kimball Jr. *Spencer W. Kimball: Twelfth President of The Church of Jesus Christ of Latter-day Saints*. Salt Lake City: Bookcraft, 1977.

Kimball, Spencer W. "Applying the Principles of Welfare Services." *Ensign*. May 1979, 98.

———. "Seagull Monument." In Conference Report. October 1970, 72.

———. In Conference Report. April 1966, 7.

———. "The Davids and the Goliaths." In Conference Report. October 1974, 112–13.

———. "Set Some Personal Goals." *Ensign*. May 1976, 46.

———. "The Role of Righteous Women." *Ensign*. November 1979, 102.

———. *The Teachings of Spencer W. Kimball*. Edited by Edward L. Kimball. Salt Lake City: Bookcraft, 1982.

———. "'We Need a Listening Ear.'" *Ensign*. November 1979, 4.

Lee, Harold B. "Stand Ye in Holy Places." *Ensign*. July 1973, 121.

———. *The Teachings of Harold B. Lee: Eleventh President of The Church of Jesus Christ of Latter-day Saints*. Edited by Clyde J. Williams. Salt Lake City: Bookcraft, 1996.

Ludlow, Daniel H, ed. *Encyclopedia of Mormonism*. New York: Macmillan Publishing Co., 1992.

Lowell, James Russell. Quoted in *That You May Have Life* by Sterling W. Sill. Salt Lake City: Deseret Book, 1974.

Lybbert, Merlin R. "A Latter-day Samaritan." *Ensign*. May 1990, 81.

Maktoum, Shaikh Mohammad Bin Rashid Al. archive.gulfnews.com, March 2000.

Maxwell, Neal A. *Deposition of a Disciple*. Salt Lake City: Deseret Book, 1976.

———. "It's Service, Not Status, That Counts." *Ensign*. July 1975, 5.

———. "The Women of God." *Ensign*. May 1978, 10.

———. *Things As They Really Are*. Salt Lake City: Deseret Book, 1992.

———. *We Talk of Christ, We Rejoice in Christ*. Salt Lake City: Deseret Book, 1984.

———. "Why Not Now?" *Ensign*. November 1974, 12.

———. "Willing to Submit." *Ensign*. May 1985, 70.

McConkie, Bruce R. In Conference Report. October 1969, 82.

———. *Mormon Doctrine*. Salt Lake City: Bookcraft, 1966.

McKay, David O. "Worth While." In Conference Report. April 1965, 81.

McKean, Michelle. "College Students' Academic Stress and Its Relation to Their Anxiety, Time Management, and Leisure Satisfaction." *Journal of American College Health.* January 1, 2000, 49:125–30.

Mendenhall, Wendell B. In Conference Report. April 1965, 81.

———. "That Faith Might Also Increase in the Earth." *BYU Speeches of the Year,* December 5, 1962, 8.

Michelangelo. quotations.com.

Miltenberger, Mayola R. "Happiness: There's Not a Single Barrier." *Ensign.* April 1988, 32.

Monson, Thomas S. *Be Your Best Self.* Salt Lake City: Deseret Book, 1979.

———. "A Provident Plan—A Precious Promise." *Ensign.* May 1986, 62.

———. "Learning the ABCs at BYU." *BYU Speeches of the Year.* February 8, 1966.

———. "Examples of Righteousness." *Ensign.* May 2008, 65–68.

———. "May We So Live." *Ensign.* August 2008, 4–9.

———. "Pathways to Perfection." *Ensign.* May 2002, 99.

———. "Tears, Trials, Trust, Testimony." *Ensign.* May 1987, 42.

———. "Your Patriarchal Blessing: A Liahona of Light." *Ensign.* November 1986, 65–67.

"Most Important Class Applauded." *LDS Church News,* June 16, 1985.

Moyle, Henry D. In Conference Report. April 1959, 98.

Nelson, Russell M. "Choices." *Ensign.* November 1990, 73.

———. "'Joy Cometh in the Morning.'" *Ensign.* November 1986, 67.

———. "We Are Children of God." *Ensign.* November 1998, 85.

Oaks, Dallin H. "Getting to Know China." BYU devotional address, March 12, 1991.

Packer, Boyd K. *Teach Ye Diligently.* Salt Lake City: Deseret Book, 1975.

Perry, L. Tom. "Fatherhood, an Eternal Calling." *Liahona.* May 2004, 69.

Petersen, Mark E. "Hear Ye Him!" *Ensign.* November 1975, 63.

Pratt, Parley P. "Do You Keep a Journal?" *The Latter-Day Saints Millennial Star.* Vol. 1, no. 6. Manchester, England, October 1840.

Richards, LeGrand. "We Have to Pay the Price." Brigham Young University devotional, October 24, 1967.

———. "Laying a Foundation for the Millennium." *Ensign.* December 1971, 81.

———. "Joy in Missionary Work." In Conference Report. April 1946, 84.

———. "What the Gospel Teaches." *Ensign.* May 1982, 29.

Rising Star Outreach. www.risingstaroutreach.org.

Robbins, Lynn G. "Tithing—a Commandment Even for the Destitute." *Ensign.* May 2005, 34.

Scott, Richard G. "Finding the Way Back." *Ensign.* May 1990, 74.

Sill, Sterling W. In Conference Report. April 1962, 13–14.

———. In Conference Report. October 1964, 13.

———. *Leadership.* Salt Lake City: Bookcraft, 1958.

———. *Principles, Promises, and Powers.* Salt Lake City: Deseret Book, 1973.

———. *The Wealth of Wisdom.* Salt Lake City: Deseret Book, 1977.

Simpson, Robert L. In Conference Report. April 1963, 54.

Smith, Hyrum M. III, and Janne M Sjodahl. *The Doctrine and Covenants Commentary, Containing Revelations Given to Joseph Smith Jr., the Prophet.* Salt Lake City: Deseret Book, 1958.

———, and Scott G. Kenney, comp. *From Prophet to Son: Advice of Joseph F. Smith to His Missionary Sons.* Salt Lake City: Deseret Book, 1981.

Smith, Joseph. *History of The Church of Jesus Christ of Latter-day Saints.* Edited by B. H. Roberts, 2d ed. rev., 7 vols. Salt Lake City: The Church of Jesus Christ of Latter-day Saints, 1932–51.

———. *Teachings of the Prophet Joseph Smith.* Selected by Joseph Fielding Smith. Salt Lake City: Deseret Book, 1976.

Smith, Joseph F. "The Returned Missionary. *Juvenile Instructor,* November 1903, 689.

Smith, Joseph Fielding. "The Thief of Eternal Life." In Conference Report. April 1969, 121.

———. *Doctrines of Salvation.* Salt Lake City: Bookcraft, 1954.

———. *Teachings of the Prophet Joseph Smith.* Salt Lake City: Deseret News Press, 1938.

———. *Teachings of the Prophet Joseph Smith.* Salt Lake City: Deseret Book, 1976.

Smith, Lucy Mack. *History of Joseph Smith.* Salt Lake City: Bookcraft, 1979.

Smoot, Reed. In Conference Report. October 1907, 57–58.

Snow, Lorenzo. *The Teachings of Lorenzo Snow: Fifth President of The Church of Jesus Christ of Latter-day Saints.* Edited by Clyde J. Williams. Salt Lake City: Bookcraft, 1984.

Spragens, William C. *Popular Images of American Presidents.* New York: Greenwood Press, 1988.

Stanley, F. David. "The Principle of Work." *Ensign.* May 1993, 44.

Taylor, Henry D. "A Time of Testing." *Ensign.* December 1971, 43.

*The International Dictionary of Thoughts.* Compiled by John P. Bradley, Leo F. Daniels, and Thomas C. Jones. Chicago: J.G. Ferguson Publishing Co., 1969.

"The Top 100: The Most Influential Figures in American History." *Atlantic Magazine*. New York: E. Bliss and E. White, December 2006.

*Times and Seasons*. 6 vols. Nauvoo, Illinois: The Church of Jesus Christ of Latter-day Saints, 1839–46.

Van Gogh, Vincent. quotationspage.com.

Walton, Sam. quotationsbook.com.

Whitney, Orson F. *Life of Heber C. Kimball*. Salt Lake City: Bookcraft, 1967.

Widtsoe, John A. *Evidences and Reconciliations*. Salt Lake City: Bookcraft, 1943.

Wirthlin, Joseph B. *Finding Peace in Our Lives*. Salt Lake City: Deseret Book, 1995.

———. "Peace Within." *Ensign*. May 1991, 36.

Woodruff, Wilford. In Conference Report. April 1898, 57.

Wright, Randal A. *Families in Danger: Protecting Your Family in an X-rated World*. Salt Lake City: Deseret Book, 1988.

———. *Family, Religious, Peer, and Media Influence on Adolescence Willingness to Have Premarital Sex* (PhD dissertation), Brigham Young University, 1995.

———. "Our Family's Reverence Lesson." *Ensign*. August 1986, 43–44.

Young, Brigham. *Discourses of Brigham Young*. Compiled by John A. Widtsoe. Salt Lake City: Deseret Book, 1976.

———. *Journal of Discourses*, 8th ed. Salt Lake City: Deseret Book, 1974.

———. *Teachings of Presidents of the Church: Brigham Young*. Salt Lake City: The Church of Jesus Christ of Latter-day Saints, 1997.

# ABOUT THE AUTHOR

Randal A. Wright received his PhD in family studies from Brigham Young University. He has worked with the Church Educational System for many years and is currently a coordinator for Seminaries and Institutes of Religion. He is the author of several books, including *25 Mistakes LDS Parents Make and How to Avoid Them* and *Families in Danger: Protecting Your Family in an X-Rated World*. He and his wife, Wendy Bradford Wright, are the parents of five children and live in Austin, Texas.